What marketing experts are saying about
Shift Happens: The New Age of Bank Marketing

"A best-of-breed bank marketer and a world class consultant have collaborated to create this year's must read for bank marketing professionals. Shift Happens is short on theory and long on practical ideas that help the financial services marketing professional to be proactive to the realities of our new economy. Most importantly, Bruce and Nick have made trust and the customer experience the centerpiece of their approach. This book will not sit on the shelf. It is a definitive filled manual to maximize your marketing and sales efforts."

Jack Hubbard
Chief Experience Officer
St. Meyer & Hubbard

"Shift Happens is questioning the old establishment and saying let's look at our customers and the experience we deliver to them a little differently – through different lenses. Marketing professionals will find this book invaluable as it leads them through an analysis of their own companies. Not only is the book thought-provoking, but it also provides real-world examples and tools to deliver these new found experiences and strategies. Clapp and Vaglio are true marketing leaders in their industry and have impacted many banks, both large and small, throughout the nation and the world."

Madeline H. Belfoure, CFMP
Senior Vice President, Retail Banking &
Marketing
Cornerstone Bank, Atlanta, GA

"*This book is an excellent, thought-provoking resource for bank marketers. It challenges bank marketers to figure out how to use technology to make the customer experience truly participative and to transform that experience into a sustainable competitive advantage.*"

Lance E. Kessler, CFMP
Lance Kessler & Associates
Mechanicsburg, PA

"*Shift Happens is an excellent resource for those new to bank marketing as well as seasoned professionals who are looking for ideas to jump start or redefine their bank's marketing program. The book contains invaluable insight into the critical elements of creating a strategic marketing plan focused on developing and maintaining a strong customer-centric sales and service culture.*"

Steve Stevenson
Executive Vice President, Sales & Service
Bank of Agriculture & Commerce, Stockton, CA

"*I liked the flow of ideas and the way it handles the current exigencies and future trends in the banking industry while revealing challenges in such an exemplary text, filled with examples and attractive motives to follow the shift.*"

Abdulrahman N. Hashem
International Accounts Officer
Arab Academy of Banking and Financial Sciences, Amman, Jordan

Shift HAPPENS

THE NEWAge

OF BANK MARKETING

How Changing Lifestyles and Customer Experience are Challenging Bank Marketers

Bruce A. Clapp, CFMP & Nick Vaglio, CFMP

Shift Happens:
The New Age Of Bank Marketing
How Changing Lifestyles And Customer Experience
Are Challenging Bank Marketers

By Bruce A. Clapp, CFMP and
Nick Vaglio, CFMP

Published by
CreateSpace Publishing
An Amazon.com Company

Library of Congress Cataloging-in-Publication Data

Trademarks
All trademarked names and products mentioned in this book are
properties of their respective owners.

Cover Design & Illustrations
Jeremy Yontz

This book does not represent the views or opinions of MarketMatch,
Inc. or Wachovia Bank, N.A., or their customers or employees.

Manufactured in the United States of America

"If you do not change direction, you may end up where you are heading"

- Lao Tzu, Chinese Taoist Philosopher

I dedicate this book to my children,
Ashley, Casey and Hailey, and to my wife, Charla,
who each allowed me the time and focus to
share my thoughts with the world.

-Bruce A. Clapp

This book is dedicated to
my wife and best friend, Diane,
and to my sons, Peter and Scott.

-Nick Vaglio

TABLE OF CONTENTS

FOREWORD

Bankers are fighting for survival and relevance in a rapidly changing world. Whether they are part of a small staff in a de novo organization or part of a multi-national financial services organization, all bankers have to face the reality that their customers are better informed, demand higher levels of service, and want more convenience than ever before.

If those issues weren't demanding enough, the pace of change in bank technology has changed the landscape forever, putting more access to banking services literally in the hands of the consumer at any time and any place. Those factors, combined with a new generation of consumers and future business leaders, have created a set of demanding challenges for bankers, as well as an equally attractive set of opportunities.

It seems like a long time ago that across the boardrooms and strategic planning sessions of large "super-regional" banks the best and brightest minds debated whether to create Internet banks. Back in those days, which was only in the mid-'90's, it seemed that only these large super-regionals could even think about delivering its products and services through the rapidly evolving world of the Internet. Predictions from that period called for, among other things, the death of branch banking and personal interactions with customers. This strategy relegated all customer interaction through technology-based platforms. In fact, some banks even began charging their customers to transact business on a personal basis in their branches.

Just as bankers' infatuation with technology seemed to be at its zenith, something interesting happened. The customer essentially thanked the banking industry for all of its efforts to serve them by using technology, but also demanded personalized service uniquely tailored to them on an individual basis. Now conversations in boardrooms and strategic planning sessions evolve around developing a customer experience and a customer-centric organization, as well as keeping up with a new mobile, and even more demanding generation, the "I" generation.

In their book, Shift Happens, Bruce Clapp and Nick Vaglio provide what can best be called a "field book" for a banker's survival during this period of rapid change and excitement. Equally as important, Bruce and Nick show the strategic importance of how a new generation of bank marketers is needed to address the changing demands and desires of bank customers.

As trained and certified bank marketers in their own right, Bruce and Nick show how important strategic marketing techniques are taken to the next level. Instead of delineating an organization's target market based on traditional demographic criteria such as age and street address, the new breed of bank marketers will need to delineate markets based on lifestyles that cross traditional generational lines.

The customer demanding mobile banking could be a 20-year old having a latte with friends at a coffee shop on Harvard Square, or just as easily be a retired couple moving funds while chatting with fellow retirees visiting their ancestral home in Ireland. The challenge for our new breed of bank marketers is "how do you market to both groups?"

As strategists-turned-authors, Bruce and Nick show the "how and why" of the generational- and customer-driven trends we are experiencing, as well as explaining what many cutting-edge organizations are doing to address those trends. Their practical approach of explanation and example provides a framework for the reader to reflect on in order to take action in their own organizations.

While surviving this period of radical change is imperative, the critical factor to thriving during this period is to develop a network of material that you can personally use to position your organization for the future. Bruce Clapp and Nick Vaglio have created such a document to begin your journey with the "I" generation.

April 2008
Gregory A. Dufour
President and Chief Executive Officer
Camden National Bank
Camden, Maine

INTRODUCTION

In this rapidly evolving technological world, the consumer has clearly transitioned to an age of "I" expectations. Today's consumer can no longer be classified as a number within a demographic category. Instead, consumers are now demanding to be communicated with as individuals. This phenomenon has created a unique set of challenges to banks and their marketers.

In late October of 1991, three unique storm fronts converged off the coast of Nova Scotia, creating a ferocious hurricane, 100-foot waves, and once in a century conditions that would reverse the jet stream, cost millions in damage and leave six men dead. Four years later, this perfect storm became the subject of a runaway best seller by the same name.

And in today's ever-changing global marketplace, there's a perfect storm of conditions that present tremendous challenges for banks and their marketing professionals. These include an overwhelming need for organic growth, shifting customer lifestyles and the growing influence of a customer experience phenomenon.

As bank merger and acquisition activities continue to diminish due to regulatory and operational issues and cost, the pressure to grow organically is of paramount importance. This is especially challenging for banks that have grown rapidly through acquisition and have dedicated precious few resources to retention, cross selling and creating advocates for their bank and brand.

In many cases, banks have become irrelevant dinosaurs. Over the last few decades, little has changed in the financial products and services available to customers today, namely checking, savings and loan products. While many banks have substantially improved operational efficiencies, some have become disconnected with their customers.

In fact, in some cases where banks have improved their delivery channels, made their processes more user friendly and improved their customer service, they have done little to improve customer loyalty and advocacy— the primary ingredients for organic growth.

Charles Darwin once said, "It is not the strongest of the species that survives, nor the most intelligent, but the one most responsive to change."

And change is constant in today's marketplace. As the global economy shifts from market driven to consumer driven, the balance of power has definitely shifted to the consumer. The power of the Internet has put the consumer squarely in control of all of their purchasing decisions. Time and place, that were once the domain of the seller, are now under the direct control of the buyer.

Consumers are no longer content simply to buy your products. They want to be collaborators in the creation of the products that fit their needs.

In the old economy, the value exchange occurred on the receiving end. Companies created products, set the price and distributed them to consumers. And the business model was to continue to study consumers and predict their demand.

Now there is a more fundamental value opportunity at the front end where consumers will pay for a more customized experience that fits their lifestyles.

While many progressive companies and banks are capitalizing on this change, others fall to the wayside. Many banks are failing to attract the 18-25 year olds that don't consider themselves to be part of the masses.

They want banks to communicate directly with them. They want their banking experiences to match their other lifestyle experiences. Banking is a means to an end for this younger generation. And as banks become less relevant to this age group they lose the opportunity to convert them to customers for life. This age group can't understand why banks aren't keeping up with their lifestyle like so many of the other companies that they have embraced.

In Pine and Gilmore's book, *The Experience Economy*, they say that it's all about creating experiences that create value for people who are starved for time.

Some major companies are capitalizing on this new wave of the future. For instance, Toyota and Nike have websites that allow consumers to design their own car or athletic shoe and have that exact single product manufactured for them. These companies have completely reconfigured their manufacturing processes to accommodate this new business model.

And many banks throughout the world—large and small—are creating unique customer experiences that appeal to a wide range of customer lifestyles.

But creating unique customer experiences isn't necessarily about expensive branch renovations and other high-profile changes. Instead, banks should focus on becoming more in tune with the lifestyles and preferences of their customers—and future customers. Then they'll be able to create unique experiences that will help to create loyal customers and advocates. It requires basic common sense combined with an ability to look beyond the horizon in order to spot evolving trends that will dictate customer preferences in the future.

The first part of this book explores organic growth, lifestyle changes and customer experience, and fully details the immeasurable impact that they will continue to have on the banking industry.

The next section focuses on the direct impact and pressures these issues put upon the bank marketing function in terms of branding, segmentation, sales management, retention and growth, and product development and pricing, among others.

Finally, the remaining section offers practical solutions, ideas and tactics specifically geared toward helping you create a sustainable competitive advantage in today's rapidly changing marketplace.

Section One

The Marketplace Shift

CHAPTER 1

Between a Rock and...

"The gods had condemned Sisyphus to ceaselessly rolling a rock to the top of a mountain, whence the stone would fall back of its own weight. They had thought with some reason that there is no more dreadful punishment than futile and hopeless labor."

"The Myth of Sisyphus"
by Albert Camus
Copyright © 1955 by Alfred A. Knopf, Inc.

Did You Know?

Morton Salt: It's never just about price

It's too easy just to give up and say "price is the only thing that matters to our customers so there's no reason to think about branding." You may believe that you work in a commodity market, but it's never just about price. Learn a lesson from Morton Salt...

Back in 1848, when Morton Salt was founded, salt really was a commodity. It was sold loose, in bags, and would quickly become hard and lumpy, especially in warm, damp climates.

It wasn't until 1914 that Morton Salt introduced a distinctive 26oz round container with a pouring spout. They dramatized the benefit of the free-flowing salt with a picture of a little girl sheltered under a large umbrella with the salt can under her arm and the now-famous slogan:

"When it rains, it pours"

This image and the slogan (which is based on an old English proverb) have been used consistently for almost 100 years.

As a result Morton Salt is the number one brand of salt in the US. For every two cans of salt sold in the US, one is a Morton Salt can, and it sells at a $0.20 price premium over other brands and private labels.

As a former Vice President of Marketing at Morton Salt said...

"The answer turned out to be simple. We found that the successful process of marketing commodities requires value added benefits... and if you are the first to add these benefits, and support them, your chances of success are far greater than if you follow someone else."

Even selling a commodity like salt, there is the opportunity to build a brand and create revenue and enduring value for the business.

Next time you hear someone saying "Our customers only ever think about price" just remind them of Morton Salt. There is always a way of creating brand value.

- *adapted from Colin Bates, **Building Brands***

Many long-term marketing professionals have undoubtedly faced their profession's version of Sisyphus at some point in their careers. In an effort to remain relevant to today's technologically savvy consumer, many financial institutions have undergone a metamorphosis from market focused, to customer focused, to out of focus.

And many have tried to appeal to fickle consumers through a relationship banking approach by creating product packages that are, at least on the surface, intended to be in the best interest of customers.

Some of these packaged products we've come across make no sense at all. Instead they look like they were haphazardly thrown together. In short, they may have been the only products that the bank could make work from an operational standpoint. They bear no resemblance to real customer lifestyle needs and most lack a compelling value proposition that differentiates them from similar product offerings from competitors. It's just another example of a good idea behaving badly.

These product packages have become banking's version of oxymoronic shopping. It would be like a tobacco company selling a carton of cigarettes with a bonus pack of nicotine patches. They just don't make sense in terms of customer preferences and needs.

Some bank marketers throw up their hands and complain that they're in a commodity business. What can they do to differentiate themselves in the marketplace other than price?

Well, there was a time when ketchup and mayonnaise were sold in large, nondescript vats, and salt was sold in large sacks. Well, Heinz, Hellmann's and Morton changed all that. Despite increased competition, price wars and countless medical reports they continue to sell tons of their products and remain market leaders.

Why do we continue to buy these products when there are cheaper alternatives? Because we have trust and loyalty for these brands. We believe that the Heinz ketchup we buy today will be as good as the Heinz ketchup our mothers and grandmothers have been buying for years.

And when competition gets intense, consumer products leaders find new ways to differentiate their product. Look at the variations of headache remedies. Aspirin was the only choice for years.

Then came buffered aspirin and remedies for children, and on and on. Relief from aches and pains was the

Insurance:	State Farm Bank, United HealthCare Bank
Retailing:	Nordstrom Bank
Investments:	American Express Centurian Bank
Credit Cards:	Capital One Bank

need. Manufacturers researched and found special consumer niches, perceived by consumers as not being filled. A little known fact is that aspirin is only manufactured in two plants in the world—the rest is marketing and branding!

For the banker, the level of competition is growing intensely. It seems like everyone wants to be in the banking business. Much of the new banking competition centers on convenience and the whole customer experience. This has long been a strong driving force for bank selection, which underscores a very basic trait of the American consumer. Add to that the belief of value added for service rendered and you have a strong force to motivate a break from traditional banking loyalty.

One quick way to break through such clutter is to make an outrageous claim—like, "We will search the entire World Wide Web for what you are looking for in less than a second"—and then deliver on that promise time after time, as Google does. This largely accounts for the success of everything from TiVo (whose outrageous promise can be expressed as "television the way you want it") to Lexus ("better than the best cars in the world").

Banking Nirvana

Getting the right product, to the right customer, at the right time, using the right channel, with the right level of service, at the right price!

Wouldn't it be great if we could do this every time? This isn't a fantasy. Many companies who firmly believe that good is the enemy of great consistently strive to make their products and services conform to the changing needs and preferences of their present and future customers. But for many banks the answer lies in developing a culture that promotes value, consistency, predictability and quality service.

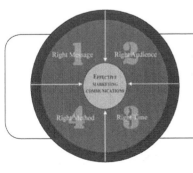

The Marketing Message Wheel is most effective when the message, audience, time and method are all aligned. It is a critical link to making banking Nirvana happen for your bank!

Banks are one of the few entities that can have a hand in helping their customers achieve their dreams, goals and aspirations. Every dream requires some level of financing, be it personal or business, to bring it to fruition. Banks and credit unions have the key to entry in helping consumers navigate through the financial maze of life.

Your challenge is to astutely determine what those goals are for each customer, and then customize a solution with the hope of ultimately creating a customer for life.

Make your customers say, "I love my bank. I couldn't have achieved these goals without them."

Chapter Keys:

1. Know your marketplace position
2. Understand your strengths
3. Identify your weaknesses

CHAPTER 2
Impediments to Organic Growth

Many banks have implemented plans to enhance organic growth, especially in challenging markets where margins are being squeezed by aggressive competitors and countless other market pressures. But as former heavyweight champion Mike Tyson once said, "Everybody has a plan until they get punched in the face."

According to an IBM Global Business Services study titled, *Unlocking Customer Advocacy in Retail Banking*, nearly 50% of customers of national banks have antagonistic relationships with their banks. That means that one of every two customers harbors an adversarial relationship with their retail-banking brand.

These customers are disinterested in developing deeper relationships with their banks, the study goes on to say, and they are also not responsive to the outreach and relationship-expanding efforts of the bank.

These customers harbor very deep and strong negative feelings toward their banks, essentially finding fault in everything that bank might do. These customers see their banks as opportunistic, self-interested parties looking out only for themselves. And this sentiment exists despite banks adding things such as service experience initiatives, implementing Customer Relationship Management (CRM) systems, and relationship programs intended to strengthen partnerships between customers and the brand.

If banks are not aware of customers' attitudes toward their organizations, and the impact these perceptions have on financial performance, they may be counting on organic growth that simply may not materialize. Worse yet, they may find actual deterioration where they expected growth.

But by identifying which customers are advocates, apathetic or antagonistic, banks can more precisely target customer experience improvement initiatives based on a more informed understanding of customer preferences and future value.

In short, banks today are simply not creating enough customer advocates—who will become excellent sources for customer referrals—or targeting influencers in their various customer segments.

Malcolm Gladwell, in his book The Tipping Point, argues that "Six degrees of separation doesn't mean that everyone is linked to everyone else in just six steps. It means that a very small number of people are linked to everyone else in a few steps, and the rest of us are linked to the world through these special few."

Research indicates that these influencers possess three important qualities—knowledge, connectivity and passion.

Why are customer advocates so important to organic growth? The IBM study also indicates that advocates, on average, hold 14% more products than antagonistic customers, and the profitability of products held by advocates is 21% higher.

Customers who are advocates of their bank are five times as likely to be responsive to offers and communications, and over 17 times as likely to trust their bank. Further, only 26% of advocates believe that their bank's fees are too high, as compared to 80% of antagonists. So as banks look to drive organic growth, determining how to move customers to a state of advocacy should be of the utmost importance.

Segment Misconceptions

A look at a typical banking customer pipeline provides insights into why few banks have been successful in creating customer advocates throughout various customer segments. While many banks are adept at identifying younger customer segments such as Youth, Teen, Gen-Y and Gen-X, they have failed to attract these segments in sufficient numbers to support future organic growth goals.

This youth market is the future lifeblood of any bank. The segment that ranges in age from 18 – 25 years old represents 30% of the U.S. population, spends approximately $200 billion per year and commands a great amount of control over household purchase decisions.

Over the next decade, the total income of this age segment will reach $3.48 trillion, putting them ahead of even the post-World War II baby boomers that have largely established their financial relationships and headed into retirement.

But why haven't banks been able to capitalize on this enormous growth potential and create young advocates? It's because banks have failed to remain relevant to the changing lifestyles of this customer segment.

On the opposite end of the banking pipeline is the segment of customers greater than 55 years of age. These baby boomers are leaving the bank in alarming numbers as some retire and move away and others switch to institutions that are in tune with their current lifestyle.

The common mistake that many banks make in targeting the baby boomers is that, unlike the younger segments, banks tend to treat the older segment as though they were one homogenous group. Viewing baby boomers as a single group fails to recognize their diversity.

Leading marketers segment this group by birth years. This method yields two subgroups: the leading-edge boomers born between 1946 and 1954, and the trailing-edge boomers, born between 1955 and 1964. According to some sociologists, the younger boomers vary so drastically from the older boomers that they constitute another generation entirely.

How important is this segment to banks? The generation of consumers born between 1946 and 1964 represents over 25% of the total population in the U.S., accounts for approximately 48% of all U.S. families, and currently controls 66% of the discretionary income in the U.S. And numerous studies have demonstrated that the level of brand loyalty among 50-year-olds is now equal to that in 20-year-olds. As such, experts assert that the brand loyalty of the previous older generations stemmed from the consolidated consumer marketplace instead of age, implying that today's baby boomers will remain open to trying new brands as long as the market contains various brand competitors.

Not only will a bank that ignores this group miss sales opportunities from spenders who may potentially switch to the bank's brand, it could also lead current baby boomer customers to feel neglected from that brand, resulting in them choosing to defect to a competitor.

Chapter Keys:

1. Know your customer segments
2. Create customer advocates that become referral sources
3. Try to identify antagonists and seek to convert them

CHAPTER 3

The Ever-Changing Customer Lifestyle

The second phase of this perfect banking storm is the profound change that technological advances have had in altering the lifestyles of consumers and putting them firmly in charge of all of their purchasing decisions.

Many banks use life-stage analysis to segment their retail customers. They use this analysis to make assumptions regarding lifestyle preferences and product offerings. But like the over-55 consumer previously mentioned, today's consumer is telling companies that they are out of touch with their diverse lifestyles and how to market to them.

According to J. Walker Smith, President of Yankelovich, Inc., "Today's consumer uses technology to participate They use it to communicate with other people and navigate through content and information. Technology has put people in complete control of the buying experience."

Accordingly, the banking industry needs to work diligently to become more relevant to its customers in light of the unique experiences they encounter in all other aspects of their lives.

Consumers are sending clear signals to companies that in order for them to buy their products and services that it had better be worth their time. And it's not that money isn't important to consumers, it's that money doesn't necessarily define value to them anymore. Time has become as valuable as money. Time has become the new currency in today's customer-driven marketplace. Transactional banking to a large degree has become a no-time activity as consumers are devaluing the simple act of banking.

People want a marketplace that is a direct parallel to their lifestyles, and one that puts them more in control over their buying experiences. The consumer wants to share their personal insights so that companies will be better equipped to serve them by responding directly to their specific needs.

Consumers don't want assumptions made about their needs and preferences. They want companies to hear their voice and to make more relevant decisions in their product development.

In a market-driven economy, the usual business practice is a top-down model that creates products based on some set of standard research assumptions. In that model, control is all about the next great product innovation. This practice contributes to a market-driven model that is an outside-in economy and a top-down marketplace.

Today's consumers, armed with information and product options, are now the movers and shakers of the new consumer-driven marketplace. And their personal preferences are the deciding factor in the choice of products they deem to have relevance to their lifestyles.

Companies that don't heed these market signals will get left behind. In a consolidating industry, such as banking, companies that continue to operate with a business model that has no relevance to the desired lifestyles of consumers stand an excellent chance of extinction. Many of the market research techniques that were used in the past to understand consumers don't necessarily apply anymore.

More and more, consumers are saying that when banks compete they win. In fact, that's the exact slogan used by LendingTree.com. Consumers are researching options online nowadays and they no longer need companies to tell them what to buy, or to give them guidance in the marketplace. Consumers have taken full control of their purchasing decisions because they have instant access to all of the necessary information required to make an informed and educated choice.

Look at companies like YouTube and Yub.com. What these entities have in common is that they are participatory. Consumers can communicate with other people and navigate through content and information. They can be part of the experience instead of bystanders to whatever degree they individually desire. Technology has put people in control. It's made life a participatory experience.

Today's average consumer with a handheld PDA can check the weather, monitor traffic conditions to their office, sell stock on Scottrade, check their Ebay bid, make a purchase on Amazon, check CNN for news highlights, transfer funds between banking accounts, check mortgage rates and get insurance quotes, all during their morning coffee.

When you see someone talking on a cell phone, using a hand held device, sending email, or clicking away on a keyboard, they are actively engaged in the activities that are most important to them.

We are living in a world where consumers have a sense of empowerment over every aspect of their life. And companies that do not engage with consumers in that way in the marketplace are out of touch with the way people live their lives today. We have to literally plug into their lives.

And in terms of lifestyle relevance and customer experience it would seem that banks are late to the dance. Consumers who have control over so many aspects of their life now demand that they also have control over their banking experiences.

Research now indicates that consumers are poised to use technology to increasingly take control of their financial experiences. They see a new model for banking where they can:
- Easily get rates and other information
- Go to a consolidation site that compiles information from scores of banks
- Get expert advice
- Get reviews from their peers

Some companies are beginning to recognize this as the wave of the future. For instance, when Toyota introduced the new Scion model, their home page carried this slogan: *We Relinquish All Power To You.*

Sure, you can still go down to a Toyota showroom and buy a car the old fashioned way. But if you want to participate in the buying experience then you can go to their website and configure your own car and Toyota will manufacture *one car just for you.* Toyota completely reconfigured their manufacturing and assembly process so that they could accommodate this new business model.

Nike offers a similar buying experience. If you want to buy athletic shoes the same old way, you can always go to the Nike store. But if you want to create your own shoe, you can go to their website, nikeid.com, and design your own pair of shoes and Nike will manufacture one pair of athletic shoes just for you. You're in charge.

Another good example is Ebay. They excel at putting buyers and sellers together, but they really don't do much of anything. They don't manufacture or distribute anything. They don't warehouse or price anything. They don't market anything. Their customers do everything by taking complete control of their own experience.

When you go to Ebay you're living a lifestyle out there in conjunction with everyone else of a similar mindset—the buying and selling of things. All Ebay does is create a tool to put buyers and sellers in touch with one another.

And if companies are not moving in the direction of empowering the consumer and involving them in the experience, then they're going to see that soon the marketplace is going to leave them behind. Consumers are revolting by saying that they will no longer just take receipt of what your company has to offer. They want to have an active role in the creation of the products that they will buy.

And that makes the company's job as a producer a very different challenge. It's no longer just about studying customers to predict what they'll do and how they'll behave. It's now about responding to what they ask for and facilitating those wishes. That's what Toyota is doing. You tell them what you want and they will make it for you. It's a very different business model.

As technology makes it easier for consumers to process and use information, we will see a shift of control in the marketplace away from companies and towards consumers. Away from centralized control and toward the feeling of decentralized control by removing time and place obstacles.

And that points to the importance of having flexibility in your marketing programs in order to match up with market realities. Companies now have to be more precise and more relevant. They have to give consumers more power and more value for their time and attention in the marketplace.

There is no substitute for profiling your best customers to gauge their personal interest and needs as they progress in age. The best computer models, MCIF or CRM systems, or other types of programs are no substitute for communicating directly with your best customers to see exactly *where* they are in their lifestyle stage.

 Many banks mislead themselves by thinking that the answers to lifestyle preferences lie in their internal data systems. Just look at this example of an employment ad for a bank market analyst.

"The Market Analyst will have the primary responsibility of maintaining the bank's customer information database. Using our MCIF system, this analyst will maximize our current information to analyze customer trends as they relate to existing and future products, as well as to identify future trends, which may include forecasting areas where future market growth is anticipated."

If you're counting on your MCIF to provide all the clues to what your customers are seeking now and in the future, then merely hiring an analyst to pore over internal customer data is not the answer. Because once a trend has already begun, then the early anticipators are the only ones who will reap the rewards.

Sure your MCIF can tell you that ATM usage has been increasing month over month for the past year. What it won't tell you is if that increase is due to customer convenience with the ATM or the fact that your bank isn't open for business when your customers want to interact with a bank employee.

It also won't tell you about missed opportunities because your customers went to a competitor who made it easier to do business with them. The lesson here is that you need to constantly talk with customers or prospects to better anticipate future needs.

An example of how easy it is to misinterpret lifestyle needs is a couple who recently bought a new house and a new car, traveled to Europe for two weeks, and paid for a semester of college. One might conclude that this couple was either in their forties or early fifties.

However, you would be way off base with that assumption. Because these are *Bruce's parents* who are both 71 years old. So you can see that in today's world, age is not a reliable predictor of lifestyle activities. You need to *listen and understand* each customer. And you need to focus marketing efforts around the 12 universal financial truths of customer life stage activities:

1. Have more money
2. Need money
3. Travel
4. Taxes
5. Retirement
6. Job Change/Life Change
7. Birth/Children/Grandchildren
8. Education
9. Death
10. Marriage
11. Housing change
12. Automobile change

Chapter Keys:

1. Make it easy for your customers to do business with your bank
2. Listen to the input of your customers either through focus groups or unpaid advisory boards
3. Create the products and services that your customers really need

CHAPTER 4

"I" Expectations

Today's consumer has a new value proposition that they are imposing upon companies who want to sell products to them. And that value proposition is that your products and services had better be worth their time. And if it's not worth their time then that company and its products have ceased to remain relevant.

In the world of *I Expectation*, value is no longer measured in material accumulation or the old values of quantity, tangibles and money, but rather in the new values of quality, intangibles and time.

In fact, time is so important that it now falls into two categories—no time or slow time. If it's not worth a consumer's time to do it then it's worth **no time**. That means that companies now have to figure out no-time solutions to all those things that aren't worth any time to consumers.

That's where technology comes into play. In a time-starved world, technology can remedy a no-time problem. But bear in mind that technology to provide no-time solutions is not something that you can charge more money for.

Continental Airlines doesn't get to charge more money because they have a nice self-service e-ticket kiosk. McDonald's doesn't get to charge more money for a hamburger because of their self-service ordering system. No-time solutions are a cost of doing business. And they don't necessarily create more value that people are willing to pay for.

Consumers don't want to spend *any* time on those things and *more* time on the things that they find meaningful. And those are the slow time activities. So if you're looking to create value in the marketplace its all about a focus on slow time experiences.

The Beringer Wine website doesn't just spotlight wine. Instead it focuses on the *five-to-nine life*. They invite you to talk about the value of time by giving tips on how to have a better experience with that time. It's all about a different focus on what creates value in the marketplace. They have inverted the *normal* model of life and brought value and focus back to the equation of their product.

If you're in the no-time delivery business, then you're a commodity business and not delivering value in the marketplace.

Pine and Gilmore, in their book An Experience Economy, say we should always ask ourselves a rhetorical question, "What would we do differently if we charged admission to come through the bank door?"

In recent consumer research on banking customers, fees were at the top of the list of things that most affects a consumer's decision on where to bank. Also high on the list was service. But consumers said that they were willing to pay higher fees if they got better customer service. It's all about the experience.

In fact, when consumers were asked in a survey what most contributed to their personal happiness it was surprising that financial security came in only at number seven. Things like personal relationships, children and time with families ranked higher on the list. It was all about the intangibles. It is about the life stage they are in, not the product that is part of the life stage. It is *your* job to figure out the appropriate product to deliver at precisely the right time.

In fact, the focus on relationships is a growing trend in the marketplace. More and more, consumers are looking for a connection with other people.

That's why there is such a huge trend in the marketplace toward social networking. An example of this is Yub.com, which is an online shopping mall. They offer things to buy from retailers such as the Apple Store, Amazon and the like. But their motto is *Meet, Hang, Shop*. They want you to meet and engage with other Yubbers. And while you're engaging with other people you'll be more likely to do business there. *Because business follows social networking, and not the other way around.*

That's why websites of this nature continue to grow because people are using technology to create a participatory experience that's not about a product. It's all about an intangible relationship that people are empowered to create for themselves.

Last.fm is a music website that compels visitors to **join the social music revolution**. They understand, like Steve Jobs did with iTunes and the iPod, that music play lists are not about personalization. They're about exchange, interaction and engagement with one another that allows personalization to come to life.

Consumers want to be part of the process. They don't just want to have access to a nice product, they want to know how its works. They want insights into the decision-making processes. They want to know what goes on in the corporate culture. They no longer are satisfied with being on the outside looking in. They want to participate in the creation of their products. They have the power because they already know what their financial options are when they walk into your branch.

The Apple store has what they call the *Genius Bar* where consumers can sit and talk with knowledgeable computer technicians that treat all customers like intelligent people. The value proposition has shifted from a *take it from me* stance to one that now says *I'll show you how it's done.*

If you go on the Mini Cooper website they have movies that show how their cars are manufactured. They are laying a foundation of trust for present and future customers.

"The boards, which usually carry typical advertising, are programmed to identify approaching Mini drivers through a coded signal from a radio chip embedded in their key fob. The messages are personal, based on questionnaires that owners filled out: "Mary, moving at the speed of justice," if Mary is a lawyer, or "Mike, the special of the day is speed," if Mike is a chef."

MiniUSA

Visit the website for Progressive Insurance and you'll see that they just don't provide their own insurance quote, but they also give you the quotes from their competitors regardless of whether they have better rates than Progressive. They have made trust a large part of their interaction with consumers. They are bringing their consumers into the loop and creating a strong bond of trust and integrity.

Chapter Keys:

1. It's all about making the experience worth the customer's time
2. Your customers already know their financial options when they walk into your branch
3. Trust and integrity are the two most important bonds you can share with customers

CHAPTER 5

The Experience Phenomenon

It seems that it's virtually impossible to pick up a business publication these days without reading something about companies that are going to great lengths to enhance the customer experience.

Many progressive companies—such as Disney, Ritz-Carlton and Starbucks—have leveraged customer experience into a competitive advantage not easily duplicated by their competitors.

Banks of all asset sizes from Washington Mutual and Umpqua to Union National Community Bank and the National Bank of Kuwait are separating themselves from the competition by following one basic tenet: it's all about the customer experience at all levels of the organization.

But bank marketers have to understand that with each brand comes a different level of knowledge or experience with that brand. In a bank, for instance, a customer who uses the branch, has multiple accounts and, perhaps, an assigned banker has a greater level of knowledge and a much different experience than a customer who merely has a checking or an online account and never interacts with a human.

Yet, each of those customer groups is important to the economic future of the bank and you need to reach them both with the same brand platform and provide them each with a tangible customer experience.

Another good example of brand-level knowledge and experience is Mercedes Benz. Maybe you've ridden in a Mercedes. Or perhaps you've visited a showroom. Or maybe you know someone who has one and they've given you rave reviews. Each of those examples represents a different level of knowledge and experience.

There was a time when Mercedes only sold three models. They've gone significantly down market and done it very rapidly. They started to run into quality problems, which was unheard of for that brand. Now they're selling everything from a $27,000 car to a $150,000 one. These two buying groups are totally different. The dealership experience wasn't keeping up with the change in the brand. And that rapid brand extension wasn't keeping up with customer expectations in terms of quality and service.

The same for banks that quickly introduce products before sales, marketing, operations, and customer service are on the same page ready to deliver a consistent customer experience.

A good example of using customer insights to help shape the customer experience is the US Bank model pictured below designed to produce relevant customer relationship strategies.

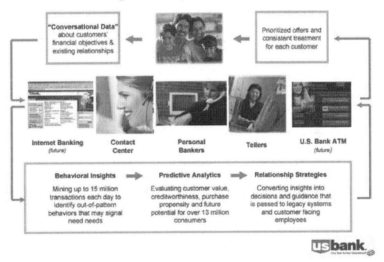

Customer insights shape the customer experience

Disney

Walt Disney was the creator of the ultimate customer experience. Through his theme parks he created a magical experience for children and adults alike that had never been seen before. He created passionate customer advocates who were only too happy to tell everyone who was willing to listen about their experience. Walt Disney shrewdly and correctly assumed that there was far greater value in getting *you* to tell his story.

He created a culture of predictability, storybook characters, friendly, smiling Disney associates that kept families visiting time and again. Have you ever seen a grumpy employee at Disney outside of one of the Seven Dwarfs?

He created the illusion of magic and the perfect vacation, and then he went to great lengths to protect it with underground tunnels for trash removal and the moving of supplies, both of which are unsightly nuisances.

Walt Disney created a predicable customer experience. Whether you went 20 years ago or yesterday, the experience is consistent.

However, despite the longevity of its success, Disney is feeling the intense pressure to keep up with changing customer lifestyles, especially at its theme park properties that are the core of its business.

A 2008 *New York Times* article about its California Adventure Park in Anaheim, California, pointed to the fact that the quickening pace of daily living, advances in personal technology and the rapidly changing media landscape are combining to reshape what consumers expect out of a theme park.

In addition, the consumer's fixation on instant gratification and personalization has been reshaping the entertainment industry for some time, but it has finally caught up to the theme park business in visible ways. For instance, Disney has spent much more effort and money developing ways to entertain people as they stand in line for rides.

"There's an erosion of patience," said Bruce Vaughn, the chief creative executive for Walt Disney Imagineering, the company's development group. "People's tolerance for lines is decreasing at a rapid rate."

More and more, younger visitors in particular, expect customized entertainment and are no longer interested in being passive viewers.

Starbucks

There was a time when you could buy a cup of coffee for 50 cents at the corner coffee shop with enough refills to keep a caffeine buzz for two days.

Then along came Starbucks. Like Disney, they also sold predictability along with a $3.50 cup of coffee. But, you know the place, even if you have never set foot in a particular store or town. It's Starbucks, and it looks pretty much like any of the thousands around the world, which is the whole idea.

The setting is familiar, yet the buzz is distinct. Starbucks has become the corner bar of the 21st century. It's become a new public space where people can go to be with other people.

Like any chain, Starbucks sells predictability. The frappuccino you order at the Starbucks in Chicago will taste like the frappuccino you order at a Starbucks in Baltimore.

And Starbucks cuts across all socioeconomic lines. After the morning rush-hour business fades, commuters give way to stay-at-home mothers and retirees, and customers with laptops. Then comes the after school crowd followed by the evening theatergoers.

They've created a new customer experience. *We're warm and fuzzy; we're familiar.* Starbucks has managed to become part of the local culture. It's not all about the coffee. Even a seemingly simple decision to add drive-thru windows to stores had to strictly adhere to the brand promise. They had to be absolutely sure that they could transfer the store experience into the vehicle. A rigorous debate was waged and processes were put into place to ensure that a consistent customer experience could be delivered.

Today, many bank marketing seminars and articles tend to focus only on the best practices and tactics that have been successful at many financial institutions, ignoring the fact that these tactics are successful because the unique culture of a particular institution is fertile ground for creating satisfied and loyal customers.

In complex intangible service businesses, such as banking, *trust* is more important than differentiation. Buyers of complex intangible services are buying specialized expertise. They are seeking an expert because they don't want to, or can't be, an expert in the service they are buying. Given a choice, they prefer to find a qualified expert they trust, rather than evaluate the expertise of many different alternatives. Again, knowledge overshadows simple information.

Most models of complex buying are rational and linear. But the buying of complex intangible services is a two-step process—qualification and trust assessment—neither of which is primarily rational.

When people buy an automobile, they have a fairly good idea of what they are buying. When these same people buy an architectural design, a customer relationship management system or a complex financial derivatives product, they are far less confident of what they are getting in return. Not only is success hard to define, so is the product itself.

Many providers of intangible services try to increase buyer confidence by stressing the differences of their particular product or service. What they forget is the biggest differentiator of all—the increased level of confidence that comes from *trust*.

And that trust is born of personal experience.

Chapter Keys:

1. **It's all about the customer experience at all levels of the organization**
2. **Make sure that all customers enjoy a consistent customer experience**
3. **Customer confidence in your brand is born of trust**

CHAPTER 6

It All Starts With The Brand

"A product is something made in a factory; a brand is something that is bought by the customer. A product can be copied by a competitor; a brand is unique. A product can be quickly outdated; a successful brand is timeless."

-Stephen King, WPP Group, London

At the root of all successful companies is a strong brand image and identity that has been carefully woven into the subconscious of consumers. There are many well-known brands that have become nouns, verbs and adjectives.

How many times have you asked someone to *FedEx* a package, even though your package delivery service provider is *UPS*?

How many times have you *Xeroxed* something on the *Canon* copier? Or asked someone for a *Kleenex* because that's what a tissue is called, isn't it?

These companies have defined an industry and represent all that is good about their product or service.

Other commodity brands like Apple, Nike and Heinz have achieved differentiation through the consumer sentiment that is attached to their unique brand. Apple is a *great innovator* that creates *must-have* products like the iPod. If you want to *play like a pro* you had better wear the Nike *footwear of champions*. And Heinz is *the ketchup that your grandmother and mother used* so it has to be the best.

Many commodity brands are readily identifiable through their brand promise that has etched customer expectations into the minds of consumers. And each has gained differentiation within their industries.

> *"Like a good neighbor."*
> *"You're in good hands."*
> *"We bring good things to life."*
> *"Can you hear me now?"*
> *"You're now free to move about the country."*

I'm sure that the majority of people would know that these companies are State Farm, Allstate, General Electric, Verizon and Southwest Airlines, in that order. And when you peel away the onion, what these companies are really saying to us is:
- "We're your neighbor, we're local. That's important when an accident or a flood occurs."
- "When you have an accident or a mishap, you will be in good hands; we'll take care of you."
- "You'll actually be able to hear the person on the other end of the line."
- "We will improve the quality of your life with great products you can trust."
- "We fly to more places cheaper than anyone else."

What could be more of a commodity than insurance? But wouldn't you want to give your business to a company that will be there to help pick up the pieces when you need them most?

If you buy a wireless phone, don't you want to hear the person you called even if it costs a few more pennies per month?

Or why should the average leisure traveler potentially spend more money to fly in the same model plane, with the same type of seat, get the same bag of peanuts and arrive at the same airport?

Where have we gone wrong?

Every time you communicate with your audience, you either build equity with your brand or you dilute it. And that means your external *and* internal audiences!

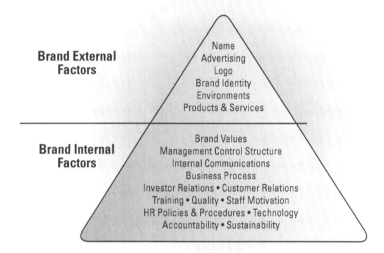

David Aaker, author of *Building Strong Brands,* said "Brand identity is the sum total of what your organization, product or service stands for—both inside and outside of a marketing context. Identity can include a variety of attributes, values, benefits, aspirations, imagery, uses, personality traits and more. But positioning is only a small part of the brand identity—the part that gets actively communicated and gives a bank leverage to influence customer decisions."

The recognition that brands now serve is much more than just an identity system can be illustrated by the concept of the "brand pyramid." The inverted pyramid concept in journalism states the most important facts first. However, many branding efforts ignore all the elements that appear below the line.   And effective brand management requires attention to critical, internal elements.

In many organizations, the entire focus centers on the external brand message and attributes and not enough attention is paid to solidifying the brand within the bank.

As a result, many branding efforts fail because of a lack of a coherent message targeted at various audiences. The internal audience has to be 100% behind the brand promise in order to build the necessary equity with the general public.

A logo is hardly a brand

A company's brand isn't created simply through the logo or corporate communications. A company's brand is built through:

-- *Products that live up to the company's claims.* Would General Electric release a defective product? Their brand and corporate culture of producing quality products that you can trust simply will not allow that to happen. Do your bank's products and services live up to all customer expectations?

-- *The public's interaction with employees.* Do you create a consistent customer experience in your branches and other dealings with bank employees like the associates at Disney World?

-- *The focus of its customer service.* Have you ever had difficulty returning something to Nordstrom? Do you resolve your customer service issues and fix the problems so that they don't recur?

-- *The company's reputation as an employer.* Would Apple discourage innovation by its employees? Is your bank the place that is admired as one of the best places to work in your community?

Ansel Adams was an American photographer, best known for his black-and-white photographs of the American West, particularly in Yosemite National Park.

Adams experimented with soft-focus, etching and other techniques of the pictorial photographers, such as Photo-Secession leader Alfred Stieglitz who strived to emulate Impressionism and tried to put photography on an equal artistic plane with painting by trying to mimic it.

However, Adams steered clear of hand-coloring which was also popular at the time. Adams used a variety of lenses to get different effects, but eventually rejected pictorialism for a more realist approach which relied more heavily on sharp focus, heightened contrast, precise exposure, and darkroom craftsmanship.

His beautiful black-and-white photographs underscored the importance that composition, texture, structure and starkness could play in evoking passions and creating lasting impressions to all who viewed his masterpieces.

Whether you are seeking to improve your brand image and message, designing your next advertising campaign or direct mail program, or creating collateral materials for your newest product, think about what you would do differently if you could only communicate in black and white. No colorful graphics and photographs, and no television advertising or radio spots to help support the core message..

In short, you would have to devote all of your energies entirely to the *message*. You would have to instill passion and a lasting impression for your brand or product in the hearts and minds of customers and prospects alike in a precious few sentences.

We recommend that you apply this *black and white* concept to your next marketing program before you add the colorful modern techniques necessary to compete for attention in today's media. You may discover that your messages will contain more relevance to your intended audiences.

Chapter Keys:

1. Make your bank's name synonymous with quality and service
2. Make sure that your own employees believe in your brand before you roll it out externally
3. Remember, every time you communicate with a customer or prospect you either build equity in your brand or you destroy it

CHAPTER 7

"If you can't explain it simply, you don't understand it well enough"

- Albert Einstein

The Brand Begins To Evolve

Branding in the financial marketplace used to be easy. Simply put up a building sign and run a few newspaper ads to notify people that your doors were now open. Everything was pretty straightforward—simple products, simple processes and simple statements.

In today's complex global economy, even a community bank located in a city of 750 people has to contend with money-center banks, brokerage houses and Internet banks, to name a few of the competitive forces in the market.

The old methods of trying to get traction in a marketplace are no longer a formula for success. The banking industry itself is partly responsible for a lot of the dysfunction found in the today's financial marketplace.

For decades, many banks followed a strategy that virtually eliminated personal contact with customers:
* Converting customers to ATM's in the 1980's
* Widespread closings of traditional branches in the 1990's
* Creation of the virtual branch via the Internet in the 2000's

Where was the ultimate wisdom in avoiding a face-to-face opportunity to speak directly with a customer to determine their needs and create a good customer experience?

Branding has evolved from a *nice touch* to an absolute necessity. In a highly competitive marketplace, banks have been forced to clearly differentiate themselves in a commodity industry. From readily adaptable products and branch networks that can be bought or sold, to the emergence of new geographic hot markets, banks have placed a great deal of emphasis on *us* versus the *market*.

Branding is clearly the means to an end for articulating a point of difference, and then ensuring that the differentiation is meaningful and sustainable. Branding, therefore, is the one single element that creates, defines and separates one bank or credit union from another.

The Evolution

Bank branding initially evolved from signage and logos to catchy taglines and phrases. That evolution continued to include a complete strategic evaluation of the entire organization in a search to find inherent attributes that could be molded into creating those experiences that matter most to customers. A classic early example of traditional branding in financial services is Bank One. Their marketing focused clearly on the organization's side of the equation.

Bank One

> *"Nine Thousand People Who Care"* -- Circa 1982
> *"Eighteen Thousand People Who Care"* -- Circa 1988
> *"Whatever It Takes"* -- Circa 1991

In 1983, Bank One purchased Winters National Bank in Dayton, Ohio, a $2 billion asset-size bank, that effectively doubled the size of Bank One. However, the Bank One name and brand eventually disappeared from the banking landscape following its acquisition by JP Morgan Chase.

Rarely in retail do you see a fabled name with a strong brand image and a faithful following simply fade away. People that appreciated the value inherent in the iconic name and what it meant in terms of quality in the motorcycle industry have resurrected Indian Motorcycles on multiple occasions. The lesson is that brands are timeless and marketing is time-based.

Unfortunately, the financial market is woefully behind the retail industry, and certainly behind the consumer, in terms of lifestyle relevance. Walk into an American Eagle store today and it is completely different than just five years ago. This is not because the retailer was eager to change, but because customer preferences dictated it.

The half-life of a wave of success in retail can be one season. For a long-lasting trend it could be a few years. Change is not only a key component to success, but rather it is the lifeline to that success.

However, we must remember that a brand is timeless and those that sacrifice their brand for a *trend* will be quickly forgotten (try to find a Benetton store!). The essence of a brand must be given precedent and steadfastly maintained. Nordstrom department stores stand for consistency and a brand promise that is timeless—the customer is always right.

For the banking industry, the saving grace is its physical distribution network. When we boil it down, banking is still very much a personal contact business where people want to interact with other people. Therefore, the brand efforts of banks and credit unions have been predominantly built around human contact positioning. Creating comfort and connection with their target market by using the same *highway*, but with many different routes.

Let's look at three common brand practices in the financial markets.
1. Brute force branding
2. Branding a place
3. Branding through service experience

Brute Force Branding

This is a common branding connection that simply throws the weight of an organization into the market and balances the brand on multiple points. Citibank is an example of brute force marketing. Citi has a tagline and brand position for each business line and day of the week.

Examples of their current taglines

Citi: *"Let's Get it Done"* • *"Live Richly"*

These are full circle from the previous tagline of "The Citi never sleeps."

Brute force branding takes the breadth of reach, the depth of organization and sheer spending to make an impact in a market or region. Larger institutional banks routinely utilize this concept that attempts to categorize the organization as a destination point versus simply an option. Similar to IBM in the technology segment, brute force marketing seeks to dominate through *in-your-face* messages with less focus on the customer experience.

IBM created the personal computer, yet very few people own IBM computers today. Awareness of IBM, however, is very high to the consumer mostly though the company's marketing efforts with large corporate clients. Brute force branding is a Goliath approach that bypasses the individual consumer in favor of volume sales.

The downfall to brute force marketing is the breadth of advertising and support needed to make it create a wave. It is truly relegated to the larger players and it creates an opportunity for more nimble players to create product or service differentiation and steal market share.

Branding a Place

Branding a place is a unique method that is more retail-like in its focus and delivery. This method attempts to focus on the delivery *place* versus the products or services delivered.

The *Occasio*TM branch system created by Washington Mutual is a classic example of branding a place. The branch incorporated a clear retail approach, especially at locations in strip-mall shopping centers. Their branch concept sought to differentiate the bank through the place of contact with the organization.

This style of branding seeks to position the physical space as the benefit of buying from the organization, and attempts to remove price, product and people from the equation. With branch banking growing at an all-time high, the strategy was envisioned to de-commoditize the branch. As the press stories grew, and the tale of the Occasio branches spread across the industry, it signaled a chase to replicate the place aspect in brand strategies.

These efforts have become a global banking phenomenon. Though this strategy is easily replicated, it is nonetheless an expensive differentiation tactic.

Branding Through Service Experience

Great quality service organizations like Ritz-Carlton and Los Alamos National Bank have turned an outstanding customer service experience into a sustainable competitive advantage. And they've been successful because employees at all levels of those organizations are empowered to be customer service ambassadors to their customers. Superior customer service is their brand. For these companies, it's not about price advantages.

Mention the Ritz-Carlton name to someone who has stayed there and superior service almost always comes to mind. When you mention the name of your bank to a customer what type of image is invoked in their mind? Is it the one that you have spent time and money on to project to your various constituencies?

Many people will counter with the argument that companies like Ritz-Carlton spend a fortune to communicate their image in a global marketplace. But if you're a community bank with a small number of branches then your operating geography **is** your global marketplace. And if you are spending 100% of your advertising and marketing budget in your community then you should, in theory, be able to solidify your image to win the hearts and minds of your customers and potential customers.

Woodforest National Bank (www.woodforest.com) is ranked among the top earning banks in the country, and is one of the largest employee-owned community banks in the Houston, Texas area. They have taken customer service and satisfaction to a new level. They were the first bank in Texas to launch a 24-hour, 7-days-a-week live banking concept and offer their customers the convenience of banking at any hour, day or night, throughout their branch network.

Woodforest has also introduced other banking firsts including seven-day processing, deposit deadlines as late as 8:00 p.m., and the development of the first *Tu Banco* branch for its Hispanic customer base.

Providing exceptional customer service has earned Woodforest the highest ranking in customer satisfaction in the Southwest Region in the J.D. Power and Associates 2007 Retail Banking Satisfaction Study[SM].

Wachovia Bank (www.wachovia.com) is a classic example of a large bank that has successfully made exceptional customer service a major component of its brand promise.

For the seventh year in a row (2002-2008) Wachovia was ranked No. 1 in the prestigious American Customer Satisfaction Index (ACSI). The report by ACSI is based on the results of an independent consumer survey by the University of Michigan Ross School of Business. ACSI surveys customers on items such as quality, value, number of complaints and the likelihood to do more business.

Chapter Keys:

1. Focus on the strengths of your organization as you evolve your brand
2. Be yourself and focus efforts on your clear points of difference
3. Broad awareness takes effort, place is easily replicated, service experience is not easily duplicated and a true remaining point of difference can be created and communicated IF you can actually deliver the promise

CHAPTER 8

The Disruptors

Today's greatest companies are those that cause an individual, or even an entire industry, to pause and ponder their organization. These firms are disruptors—ones that create an impact by disrupting the commonly held thoughts and beliefs within an industry and then, by virtue of their existence, change the landscape of that industry forever.

Disruptors have had a historical impact that cannot be ignored. Some, like eBay, have become industry icons. Other companies such as De Lorean automobiles have simply faded away. Yet regardless of their fates, the fundamental lessons and impacts of these companies last for ages.

Another example is Skype. Before 2003, no one had ever heard of this company or its product offerings. However, in two short years, it completely changed the landscape of telecommunications.

Skype is a software program that was created by Swedish and Danish entrepreneurs and a team of software developers in Tallinn, Estonia. Skype allows users to make telephone calls over the internet to other Skype users free of charge, and to non-Skype landlines and cell phones for a fee. Additional features include instant messaging, file transfer, short message service, video conferencing and an ability to circumvent firewalls.

The Skype Group, acquired by eBay in September 2005 for 3.4 billion Euros, has experienced rapid growth in both popular usage and software development since its inception. In 2006, there were 100 million registered users. By the end of 2007, that number had grown to 280 million users. At that time, Skype accounted for over 5% of all international carrier traffic.

Skype application icon through the years

2003   2003   2004   2004   2004   Today

This is a timeline of how the Skype application icon has evolved through the years.

A banking example of a disruptor is Umpqua Bank (www.umpqua.com), headquartered in Eugene, Oregon, with offices from California to Washington state. Umpqua went from one branch in 1953 to become one of the leaders in a customer experience revolution in 1995. Its differentiation strategy became a disruptor within the banking industry.

Umpqua's marketing and branch retail approach is as unique as it is different. Focused on shifting the concept of banking from the bank to the consumer, Umpqua delivers an experience that engages the consumer, removes price from the equation and replaces it with place, product, people and relevant promotion. Although Umpqua reaches out beyond the branches to touch consumers, it successfully utilizes its branches as a central gathering place to personally connect with the community.

In 2008, Umpqua launched an Innovation Lab at one of its branch stores to experiment with new strategies, service tactics and methods to engage their customers. In true Umpqua style, it is as much about the community and the people as the bank. Check it out at www.umpqualab.com.

From Umpqua's website:

Any company can have a slogan. In fact, most do. But are they true to their words?

When we say "Welcome to the World's Greatest Bank," it's more than an expression, more than a slogan. It's our commitment to our customers and communities, and it's our commitment to ourselves. It's the reason for everything we do. Whether you're visiting one of our stores, or visiting us online, we want to provide you with an environment and a feeling that you couldn't match anywhere else. It's a place where you can find all the services of a larger bank, while enjoying all the comforts of your neighborhood store.

We need disruptors to keep us all on our toes and view life from a 360-degree perspective. Disruptors have the envious role of leading from the front of the line, and the arduous task of carving out change as they go. It is a tough road, but a potentially profitable one. And it takes energy, focus and commitment that go far beyond the rational realm in which most companies operate.

The key element of being a disruptor is:
 • Think "out of the box" on "in the box" items
 • Create fundamental change
 • Empower staff
 • Engage your customer

In today's ever-changing marketplace, a true *disruptor* needs to be a focused agent of change with the foresight and vision to meet the future needs of customers.

It is certainly possible for your bank to be a disruptor either in your market or for your customers or employees. And it doesn't necessarily have to be on the scale of a Skype or an Umpqua.

There are three models of disruption that we encourage you to consider in order to determine how they may apply to your unique situation:
 1. Industry
 2. Marketplace
 3. Internal

Industry

This is the most challenging type of disruptor. This is a top-down model that is dictated down through the organization. It influences every decision and move the organization makes. It focuses on changing the rules, and that begins to cause a shift in the thinking and actions of the entire industry. Industry-changing companies include Skype, Umpqua and Wal-Mart. These companies are game changers on a broad spectrum.

Marketplace

This is a model that encourages creative thinking in your delivery and interaction with customers and prospects. The marketplace disruptor causes people to shift their buying patterns and their thought-making processes.

Just like JDs Custard shop changed the perception of ice cream and service in Englewood, Ohio. By revitalizing a centuries-old recipe to focus on the community, JDs forced a change in how, when and where people buy ice cream. They differentiated themselves by focusing on a base product and making incremental, high-quality improvements and changes over a period of time based on customer demand.

A good example of a financial services disruptor is Florida Commerce Credit Union. They have become a leading auto lender in Tallahassee, Florida. They have managed to change the lending landscape in their community through ease of transaction, the quality of their staff and a broad outreach program for car buyers.

Internal

The internal disruptor model causes the staff to look at the world through the eyes of change. The ripple effect is determined by how the staff interacts with customers, the decisions they make with regard to problems and complaints, and how the organization is structured. The most important aspect is senior management's daily interaction with front-line staff. The more the interaction, the closer to an internal disruption model the organization becomes.

The amount of disruptive force in the marketplace is in direct correlation to the flatness of a company's organizational structure. This is critical because then the staff begins to fully understand the direction and focus of the organization. They will also feel empowered to make things happen and hopefully be rewarded through better customer loyalty and deeper relationships.

Chapter Keys:

1. Learn from disruptors in other industries. Their approach, process, implementation, etc. are key milestones to analyze
2. Determine how you can be a disruptor in your marketplace?
   a. Products?
   b. Service?
   c. Locations?
   d. Promotions?
3. Ensure that self analysis and creative thought are encouraged and fostered, it leads to positive disruption of the status quo

Section Two

The Internal Shift

CHAPTER 9
Making Marketing Relevant

Marketing is a critical function in nearly every industry. Crafting a message that sells a product, presents a service or convinces people to act is one of the fundamental necessities in a free-market economy.

However, for the typical bank or credit union with assets under $1 billion, the marketing function has many times become an afterthought. This is a troubling trend considering that this asset segment represents nearly 90% of all banks and credit unions in the United States. You also see this trend in many de novo-banking situations.

Marketing needs to find a place at the executive table and be known internally as the "go-to" function for customer and market impact. Mainly, you need to raise your place from "artsy design and parties" to sophisticated strategic thinkers that guide and implement key strategy and tactics for the institution. So, how do you get that evolution to begin?

Despite the best operational policies, procedures and plans, many banks are still failing to attract the most profitable customers. As outlined by E. Jerome McCarthy, professor of Marketing at Michigan State University, and author of the book *Basic Marketing*, marketing is made up of the four Ps—product, place, promotion and price. Philip Kotler further popularized these principles.

These are the building blocks for making marketing matter. However, adding a new level of strategic thought will require even more focus and delivery to ensure that marketing is seen as an investment in the organization versus merely a cost/expense center. ROI will be a key metric for all marketing output.

Marketing's most fundamental role is to match customer needs with the most appropriate product or service of the organization. Marketing at its best should be capable of creating interest, inciting passion and moving people to action. In a commodity business, such as banking, marketing is necessary to educate the customer about financial information and to provide them with the value that will differentiate one bank from another.

For maximum effectiveness, marketing must deliver three things in the internal environment of the institution:

1. Uniqueness
2. Relevance
3. Sustainability

These elements help give the marketing department credibility within an organization and help it to overcome the stigma that it is simply the place to send all unclaimed mail or the place to call when someone needs more pens with the bank logo. By ensuring that your marketing remains unique, relevant and sustainable, you can then leverage the energy of the entire organization, increase communication and help to lift the results of your bank. This translates into action, planning, integration and delivery.

Uniqueness

Defining the impact of marketing can be a major challenge. Marketing doesn't produce any products, directly touch the sales process or interact with the customer after the initial sale. So, what do you do? You make all of those things happen! Marketing is the engine that drives performance.

This is a unique position, and one that requires balance, communication, planning and skillful delivery. You must also be the face of the organization and a major contributor to growth and change. Understanding the strengths and weaknesses of both the organization and the marketing strategy supports that uniqueness. The important lesson here is to make your message uniquely your own in order to increase the receptivity of the audience.

Uniqueness is also critical to your external marketing programs. In Dayton, Ohio, there is a carpet retailer called Buddy's Carpet Barn. It is a dynamic organization that is the leading carpet retailer in the area, ahead of established retail giants. In fact, they are selling more carpets than competitors with multiple outlets. How do they do this? The owner's name is Buddy and his advertising is focused on giving the customer a "buddy in the carpet business." Although it might be perceived as being cheesy, sappy and low-cost, it has been one of the most effective messages in the marketplace! Why? It is unique and everyone remembers Buddy! And, in the last measurement of truly effective uniqueness, it translates into carpet sales!

Relevance

In most organizations the key to relevance can be directly attributed to a contribution to the bottom-line. And to your CEO, that bottom-line relevance directly translates into some pre-determined multiple of the marketing department's expenses. The old ROI conundrum rears its ugly head again!

The marketing department must continually demonstrate that it is a creator of sustainable value, and not simply a consumer of time and budgets. Communication is fundamental to being organizationally relevant as you position the marketing department to be a creator of profitable actions, strategy, tactics and results.

The next step is being relevant to the customer. And that means staying in tune with their lifestyles and needs, and to remain fully integrated with their preferred methods of acquiring information. Customer and prospect targeting is the foundation of relevance, because relevance is a moving target when it comes to your customers.

True relevance evolves with your customers. It changes from customer to customer in how products and services are delivered through the appropriate channels exactly when they are needed by the customer. The right message, to the right customer, at the right time, using the right channel defines relevance. How do you determine the variables to this equation? You do it through research! You must talk with your customers to find ways to gain insights into their needs, and then funnel that information directly into your marketing planning.

But research is only part of the relevance dynamic. The true magic of the research is incorporating the findings into your daily activities. You must find tactical ways to make your research come alive in order to make a relevant impact on your customer. It may be as simple as understanding that the reason an ATM is underutilized is that there is a low level of light surrounding the ATM that engenders a feeling of insecurity.

Rectifying this ATM situation has direct relevance to the customer. Not to mention increasing the ATM transaction levels! From a product perspective, it could be recognizing the impact that grandparents have on the savings habits of their grandchildren. Making your children's savings account product have a clear connection to grandparents will help to make the account more relevant and timely.

Sustainability

Like the Morton's Salt story, marketing must be the key player in helping to build a competitive advantage that is sustainable through any market condition over an extended period of time. You must be the key driver in creating advocates for the brand at all levels of the bank in order to maintain a sustainable competitive advantage.

From its first opening day in October 1971, Disney World has sustained its competitive advantage through intensive training, constant communication and a clear purpose. From the lowest level employee to the highest executive, Disney has created a focus on sustaining an image and perpetuating a method of delivery. Your institution needs to have the same fervor and focus to ensure sustainability of your purpose.

And do not confuse sustainability with either invincibility or inflexibility. The railroad industry is a constant reminder of those latter two traits. They lost sight of being in the transportation business, and their sustainability waned when their uniqueness and relevance was lost.

Sustaining a competitive advantage in a commodity business requires that equal effort be given to solidifying the main messages to both internal and external audiences.

Sustainability is as important to delivery as to the actual product. Have you ever visited a restaurant that was new to the area? At first, the portions are large, the service and the food are excellent and the customer experience is outstanding. However, while the food quality may remain excellent over time, the portions begin to shrink, the service gets spotty and the value of the experience becomes greatly diminished.

The key to sustaining a loyal customer relationship is to treat every day like it's "Opening Day!" Opening day always has the high energy and the clear focus of everyone. Sustaining that competitive edge takes systems, processes and accountability. And the marketing department should be the engine that drives the accountability of the organization. You <u>have to be</u> the voice of the customer!

Chapter Keys:

1. Find your unique points as a marketing team and align them to your organization's strengths and abilities
2. Relevance is only gained by going to the source. Create ways to capture information and integrate it to your planning and delivery
3. Sustainability is established and maintained as a result of uniqueness and relevance Your future depends on your ability to position marketing and make an impact

CHAPTER 10
Marketing As A Philosophy

In many low-performing organizations marketing is viewed as a group of artsy types focused on creating advertising and brochures. In high-performing organizations, marketing has formed strong partnerships with groups throughout the organization including business development, sales, operations and executive management who all recognize the intrinsic value that marketing brings to the dynamics of the bank.

In these organizations, marketing has become the conduit to understanding the needs of customers and translating that information throughout the organization in order to grow existing relationships and acquire new customers.

A first sign that marketing has become a philosophy within an organization can be understood simply by listening to the pronouns that employees use. If they use words like "we," "us" and "our", then the marketing department will have limited influence within your bank. However, if employees use words such as "they" or "them," then the marketing group can have a major organizational impact.

As a marketer, your role is to be an agent of change. With a constantly shifting economy, customer base and staff changes, a marketer has to set the tone and lead the charge. This change starts with a four-step process designed to get you out of the marketing chair and into the front of the room.

The critical four-step process is:
1. Engaging
2. Listening
3. Empowering
4. Communicating

By following a clear strategy, you can begin to mold marketing into a powerful approach and move the organization forward, and, at the same time, move your career forward. It begins with your razor sharp focus on a strategy that evolves into tactical delivery and uses the four-step process to involve the entire organization.

Engaging

As a marketer, you need to understand all areas of the institution, its issues, challenges and methods of success. Once you understand how the bank functions and makes money, you can further articulate strategy and tactical input to drive the relevant "triggers" of the bank. Your best friend should become the CFO who is the gateway to financial information and knowledge about the bank and the current and expected future position.

A greater understanding and engagement of the financial structure of the bank will provide you with key insights into asset allocations, pricing fluctuations, income drivers, and how the balance sheet is overall managed. These are all key fundamental insights into knowing the what and when to promote certain products and services and to maximize certain segments.

The second step of engagement is the staff. All organizations are more effective when marketing's influence transcends to the entire organization. However, this transformation is nearly impossible without an engaged and involved staff, especially the front-line customer facing staff. You must find ways to seek their involvement, engage them into the process, detail how their position and input impacts the overall bank and the marketing efforts, and finally encourage them to share insights they are learning everyday about customer behavior, needs, and reactions to products and services.

Listening

In many organizations, everyone fancies themselves a marketer, or, at least, a critic of marketing's output and strategy. When you develop methods to engage people you must also have an ear for listening. If you elicit staff feedback and then are perceived as being inattentive, people will cease to provide imformation and remain engaged.

However, it is imperative to remember that while the staff are providing insight, feedback and information, the final decisions regarding the marketing strategy, direction, budget allocation, etc., must remain with you. A helpful reminder of that proper flow and separation of duties is important. You do not want to project an image of passing the buck or allowing everyone into the decisions. It is a balancing act that you need to master!

As Bruce's father always said, "you have two ears and one mouth. Use them in proportion!" You must do the same. Engage people and then take a step back and truly listen to what others are saying. It may be a bit painful if they attack the ads you created, but keep in mind your goal is the best marketing deliverables based on the clearest understanding of the overall bank strategy. Sometimes, you cannot get there yourself and you need the help! Accept it and provide feedback on its value and use.

Empowering

In an organization of 200 people with a marketing team of three, you have only three voices to ensure that your marketing focus is correct if you eliminate staff involvement. If you can empower others in your organization to accept and lead marketing support ideas or to be your regional representative for implementation, then you can leverage the team of three voices into a choir of 200 voices! Which would you think is more successful? We agree...the choir of 200!

Empowering people is another balancing act. You must empower people to act, respond and share when it comes to marketing. However, you must maintain control of the brand promise and brand delivery to ensure consistency is at the core of all actions. While it is prudent to empower people with added responsibilities, accountability always should stay with you! Empowerment needs to involve the staff person and their manager to make sure that you are not overstepping job boundaries, and to get the buy in that's necessary to support the initiatives or responsibilities you have empowered people to participate in.

Communicating

Communication, as you undoubtedly know, is a major source of empowerment. Knowing the strategy, hearing inside information on a program's goals, and being involved from the initial start of a strategy, is very empowering for the staff. It engages them to assist in creating the solution while ensuring a feeling of ownership in the process and results.

Communication must occur at all levels of an organization, and there is certainly a point of both relevance and appropriateness to your communications. It is relevant and appropriate to share program strategy, targets, goals, and success rates with all staff. It is not relevant or appropriate to share such things such as cross-departmental incentive rates, etc. Communication should be short, to the point, at regular intervals, and broadly delivered. Items to communicate include program progress, goal changes, strategy insight, and key details on targets or segments. Targeted communication is the payoff for the staff feeling engaged and empowered. It also demonstrates that you are indeed listening to the team!

The goal for every marketer should be the knowledge and feeling that your team is just as involved as you, and that they are thinking strategically to complement your ideas, thoughts and actions. Then you will know that you have crossed into the nirvana of marketing philosophy with you as the agent of change versus simply being a marketing department.

Chapter Keys:

1. **Marketing is more effective when you move from a marketing department to having an organizational philosophy of marketing**
2. **There are four (4) critical steps for you to employ that can assist your efforts in creating a marketing philosophy**
3. **Communication is the ultimate payoff for those that believe in a marketing philosophy, be sure to reward the team with key information and insights**

CHAPTER 11

Developing An Internal Culture

Your institution has an external and internal culture. Knowing the key differences, and ensuring that your internal culture is defined, refined, and aligned with your goals is the key to success.

Your external culture encompasses, among other things, your reputation, your brand and the collective experiences of customers. Your internal culture is based on the mindset of the staff, the philosophy of managing the work force, and the focused goal of the organization.

The institution's culture is the environment that either creates and expands behavior, or stifles and constricts behavior. Regardless of what you may think, *every organization has a culture.* Similar to water that will always find its own level in any given situation, an institution's culture will permeate all levels of an organization whether it is encouraged or not.

An inherent danger in ignoring your existing culture is that it may not be a culture that will enable your bank to be successful in your market!

A clearly defined culture starts with the executive management, is refined and defined by senior management, clearly managed and reinforced by the front-line management, and implemented every day across every department and function by the front- line staff. A culture helps define the "moment of truth" of how decisions are to be made, what variables are acceptable, and how the communication will occur.

So what exactly is a culture? We will define it simply as the silent guiding force that models actions, guides decision making, and acts as an operating principle for the staff and the organization. Examples of company cultures across several industries:

- Apple- innovation and breaking paradigms
- Nordstrom- Yes, the customer is right
- Southwest Airlines- work hard, have fun, do it right
- ESPN- looking at life from the sports enthusiast's chair
- Umpqua Bank- innovation designed to get closer to the customer leads all priorities

Each example illustrates a culture that manifests itself in the "how," "why," "when," and "with what speed" decisions are made. Apple and its employees don't stop being innovative based on the constraints of existing technology. They constantly evolve their products and technology to meet the perceived needs of their customers.

How are decisions made in your institution? From the customer viewpoint? Ensuring it is currently operationally feasible? To improve profit? To gain more customers? Are new hire decisions made at the branch level or at HR level? Are new employees merely sent out to fill the position? Each is very telling about your culture.

So how do you develop, influence, redefine or change your culture? Easy. Just go flip the "culture change" switch on the wall (don't you wish it were that simple!) In reality, your culture changes and is reinforced on a daily basis. The key variables to establishing or developing your culture revolve around four areas:
- The leadership at the CEO and board level
- The leadership at the Senior Management level
- The leadership at the customer level
- The inspection of expectations at the staff level

A culture needs daily upkeep and constant vigilance to ensure it takes hold and evolves in the direction that supports the goals and vision of an institution.

Board/CEO Leadership

This is where the cultural tone of an organization is set whether it is sales centric, customer service driven, or customer centric. A culture is not simply a "memo" that mandates behavior or outlines expectations; it must come with support, definition, mentoring and constant vigilance to be successful.

Even the best teams composed of the top individual talent need a great coach to put them on top. The Board and CEO must articulate the culture through policy and, more importantly, through accountability that supports the desired outcome. If your organization does not have a Board-CEO leadership focus that creates and defines your internal culture (or at least one that assists in supporting a marketing philosophy) then it is imperative that you communicate the issues and the challenges of the internal environment upward to the Board and CEO, a process that can be fraught with pitfalls. Be sure to keep to the facts, demonstrate the challenges from an organizational perspective, and be ready to offer a potential solution (always address challenges with a potential solution in mind.)

Senior Management Leadership

Senior management is the lightning rod for cultural change within an organization. They act as the company mentors and ultimately are accountable for a culture taking root. All areas must be in alignment toward the cultural goal. Think of a car engine. If even one of the cylinders is off in timing or effectiveness the overall horsepower is diminished and a "pinging noise" is heard. In your bank, that pinging noise may be high employee turnover or continued missing of revenue goals. Senior management must be quick to diagnose and intercede for a successful culture to grow and be nurtured within an organization. It must have a voice and a consistent application for success.

Customer-Level Leadership

Customer-level leadership is where the rubber ultimately meets the road. Your culture lives or dies everyday when your institution interacts with a customer at any touch point. It could be online banking, the call center, a branch, or simply through a piece of correspondence. The customer-level leaders have to ensure that each and every interaction and customer contact is held to the standards of the culture.

This leader level is maximizing its full power and influence when it ensures that focused attention is placed on the importance of the customer experience, immediate action is employed when challenges arise, and adequate support is delivered to the customer.

The customer level is the single greatest point for collecting data and assembling the impact and success of a culture. If it is defined, refined and aligned to match customer needs with the abilities of the organization it will result in increased sales, soaring satisfaction, and staff that begin to migrate from jobs to careers.

On the customer side, loyalty improves, relationship depth expands, and referrals are increased. These are measurable and quantifiable variables that dictate success, failure or the need for intervention on the different leadership levels. This leads to the fourth and final step in developing an internal culture.

Inspect What You Expect

Close inspection of progress is the lynchpin that will determine success or failure for an institution. Marty Cohen, CEO of Cohen-Brown Sales Management, has always prophesized the concept of "Inspect what you Expect." Considering that Marty is a former psychiatrist and expert in human behavior, truer words have never been spoken about your staff culture.

In sociology, there is a proven theory of communities that deals with a "broken window" at a property. If a community always fixes a window when it is broken, then everyone continues the same behavior and the community is vibrant, is in good repair and moves forward. If, one time, the window is not fixed at a home, the second property where it occurs is greatly influenced by the inaction, and soon the entire neighborhood falls into disrepair.

How does your institution deal with staff behavior, actions and meeting expectations? High performers will typically always outperform other employees in any market environment. However, if they constantly are surrounded with people that do not meet expectations and where there is no corrective actions or consequences, they will also ratchet down their performance levels. This is, assuredly, counterproductive to your goals!

Remember, your internal culture defines your external culture. Your internal culture will impact the experience your customers receive and your ability to attract, retain and grow relationships.

Chapter Keys:

1. Understand the difference between your external and internal culture
2. Define the internal culture that will provide the best success for the organization
3. Follow the four steps in creating, defining, refining and aligning your culture with the realization that it is a process that takes time to and effort to install or change

CHAPTER 12
Examining Your Experience

Part of the entire "inspect what you expect" process is the quantification and classification of the customer response to your experience as an organization. As we discussed in the last chapter, there are definable metrics that you can evaluate to:
- See how your institution is performing
- See where issues impacting the experience may be created
- Help to identify areas of concern or elation

In this evaluation process the customer response is the collection of their experiences with your organization. The "experience" of your customer at all contacts points (telephone, website, ATM, in person, through mailed information, etc.) defines the impact of both your internal and external culture. It is measured in impact, awareness, and effectiveness. The experience is a reflection of your brand and absolutely has to be in alignment with your brand promise. If your promise is "The Best Bank in the Midwest," does your experience reflect that promise? From your brochures and staff in office, to your direct mail and facilities, from your website to your mailed notices and everything in-between, your experience directly impacts your ability to support your brand, grow the bank and service your customers.

It is not a stretch to say that your experience will directly impact your ability to cross-sell. While a customer will probably not decline a home equity offer because your brochures are not properly branded or confusing, it certainly will impact their perception of your organization. Your first step in examining customer experience is the experience audit.

An experience audit will tell you what, where, when, how, and why your customer has developed their feelings toward your institution. It will confirm whether your internal culture has created a memorable, positive experience or a disappointing, poor experience. A few signs of a poor culture and poor experience are:

- It takes four transfers of a customer phone call to receive an answer to a question
- Your website is difficult to navigate and the abandon rate is high on certain web pages
- Your loan process is cumbersome and challenging to understand and leaves customers frustrated due to a lack of information

A few signs of an aligned culture and positive experience:

- The staff accepts ownership of customer problems and shepherds them through the organization until resolution
- Your communications are clearly tied to your brand promise and constantly reflect and reinforce your mission and goals
- Processes are constantly reviewed for ease of use and customer focus

These signs are everywhere whenever a culture is either acting poorly or in line with its intended goals. The key difference is looking around with your customer eyes and being brutally honest in your assessment. This is far better than customers' brutal action of leaving your institution based on their poor experiences.

The easiest audit to perform is at the branch level. Pull into the parking lot of a local branch. What do you see? Trash, potholes in the parking lot, barely visible parking stripes? Walk in the front door. Is there still a sign that says we will be closed on President's Day when it is now April 1? Are the hours listed on the door readable? Are they correct? When you walk in the branch, is it clear where to go to ask questions? Does the lobby and the teller line look inviting or straight out of a 1970's B-movie? These are simple questions that not only define your customer experience but directly impact your staff's ability and success rate in cross-selling, attracting and retaining customers.

The experience audit should be a routine process that provides a constant monitoring of your experience delivery. From a clearly defined set of expectations for action and appearance, it should be a weekly review from front-line management, as well as a monthly or quarterly review by senior management. Marketing should be a driver of the experience audit content and definitions. The experience audit should include areas such as:

- Physical appearance of the facilities
- Upkeep of all customer materials
- Evaluation of the time required for different customer actions to be delivered
- Delivery of the brand promise
- Interaction of the areas with other internal areas/functions
- Ease of use and interaction with the department/function from the customer perspective

This first step in evaluating customer experience is the crucial building block of the process. It sets the baseline and then measures against it for positive growth and impact. You will have created a measuring stick for progress and, most importantly, for measuring the institution from the perspective of the customer. To that end, you need to further refine and define what customers want and need by category and how the experience may need to be delivered accordingly (all in alignment with your brand promise!). One method is to categorize your customers into four distinct smaller buckets.

Experience by Category

You can group your customers into four experience classifications, based on a time continuum: new, existing, exiting and exited. This simple categorization helps you to determine the potential timeframe for when customers could start to become disillusioned with their experiences, and it also provides a guide for experience modifications. By applying a time/value function to all customers, it helps to focus your efforts and to create a clear next-step plan for action.

The following illustration demonstrates the categories and the axes of customer value and time. Ideally, the customer value should increase over time. If the customer is disillusioned with the experience, the impact will be felt through attrition and lower balances and, ultimately, on the bottom line of the institution.

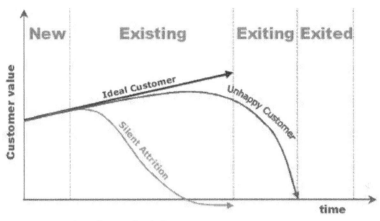

Adapted from Genroe Pty. Ltd.

By analyzing your customer base and clearly assigning a category of behavioral value, you begin to align a foundation of process points that can improve the customer experience for each sector. For instance, a new customer's need for a complete immersion into the bank and a total experience is greater and different than a customer that has been with the bank for five years. The former needs more information about how the institution fits their lifestyle and to navigate to get assistance. The longer-term customer has a need for the next solution in their financial evolution and the right financial advisor to assist with that progression.

New

Understanding customer expectations and matching them to the bank's skill set or delivery is the key factor in successfully integrating customers into the organization. A technique that has been successful in assimilating customers into a bank is using an onboarding process. Activities associated with this process are designed to create an immediate connection to a customer and a greater initial relationship depth.

For example, moving your staff from simply providing an ATM location brochure to a customer to mapping out ATM locations that are convenient to that customer's office or home, is a simple, yet effective, way of providing added value. Clear steps and actions that define our experience in the new customer stage are important for creating an immediate relationship with your customer.

Existing

Often, after welcoming a customer to the organization, many banks then allow the relationship to fall into a pattern of basic service and communication—the simple monthly statement and branch visits. You must evaluate the relationship of your existing customer base and determine how you can consistently and effectively provide value to the customer relationship. Invitations for coffee from the branch manager, special receptions for customers and anniversary notes are simple and easy methods to stay connected with your existing customers. Remember, your customers are your competitor's top prospects!

Exiting

Exiting is the beginning of the end of a relationship. This is the stage where a good customer experience is perceived as less frequent, less impressive or less valuable in the eyes of your customer. You have become less relevant to their financial life and may have allowed a competitor to begin eroding their relationship with you. At this point, customer experiences need to be reinvented and redefined for the exiting customer or you will lose them and their total relationship. Communication is an important key as well as improving the number and frequency of touch points with the customer.

Exited

These customers have already left your institution because the experience failed to meet customer expectations. At this point, you need to evaluate both the institution and the departed customer. You need to know the reasons for their departure before you can enact corrective measures. Where did it begin to falter? What can you do to improve customer relationships?

The most telling variable in the data examination of customer experience is their overall behavior. Are your customers:
1. Expanding?
2. Declining?
3. Maintaining status quo?

The key here is to develop insights of customers in these three categories. Here is a quick diagnostic tool at the different levels.

Expanding

This represents a deepening customer relationship compared to your benchmark analysis. The expansion can occur at either the individual targeted customer level or organizationally. Expanding at the targeted customer level will mean more of those customer types, or more products, services or balances by those targeted households. An organizational expansion would be represented by a greater initial cross-sell ratio, higher account balances, a broader use of all services and longer ownership of your products.

Declining

This is where customer relationship depth is decreasing. This can be in total numbers of households, accounts or depth of services used. At the customer level it could mean fewer accounts or services per household, or declining balances. At the organization level it could include slower or negative customer acquisition growth. It can also mean fewer transactions in service categories (i.e. fewer debit card transactions per customer or fewer deposits per month).

Status Quo

The status quo is little or no movement in any categories including relationship depth, balances, services used, or transaction per service type.

Understanding the impact of the various customer modes is crucial to diagnosing the issues present in your customer experiences. Matching the data with the experience audit tells you what, specifically, is attributing to the customer experience being below expectations.

Chapter Keys:

1. Audit your customer experience from the viewpoint of the customer
2. Realize the experience is a collection of all touch points; therefore all touch points must be evaluated and measured
3. Categorize your customers by the mode and behavior to help determine where and when the experience is being negatively impacted

Section Three

The External Shift

CHAPTER 13

Creating Competetive Advantages

Creating a meaningful value proposition

Once you've established your brand with internal and external audiences, you can then begin the process of translating the brand message into a value proposition that is consistent and relevant in the marketplace.

The value proposition is meant to communicate that you are prepared to offer the products and services that are in the best interests of the customer to help them grow and prosper. And it is the first key step on your way to creating a sustainable competitive advantage.

This is especially critical in today's competitive marketplace where the big banks now want to mimic the community banks and vice versa, as demonstrated in the following graphic:

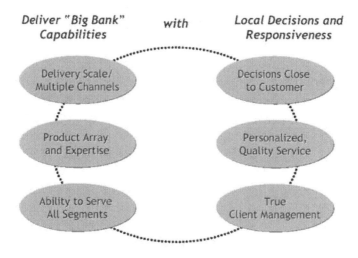

However, in this rush to reposition themselves in the marketplace, many banks—both large and small—have fallen prey to what we like to refer to as *good ideas behaving badly.*

Sample some of the value propositions that are currently being used today:

- We value our clients, and like to build lasting relationships, today, tomorrow, together.
- Its all part of what we call relationship banking
- We believe the key to success is a close working relationship with our customers
- You'll find everything you need in a full-service business banking relationship

The only thing missing from these statements is to all join hands and sing *Kumbaya*. These are not value propositions. They are business-card slogans, annual report themes, something the bank CEO's wife came up with at 3 a.m.

A value proposition needs to be just that: something that communicates to the customer that you bring *value* to the relationship in terms of products, customer service and informed advice. A bank's greatest assets go up and down the elevator every day. So using that analogy, what value could a banker convey to a customer or prospect if the banker had only 30 seconds (the length of an elevator ride) to deliver the bank's value proposition?

An excellent example of a value proposition—or 30-second elevator conversation—that is currently being used by a bank revolves around people, service and ideas:

People

- Talented, experienced local bankers and relationship specialists backed by a team of product partner specialists
- Access to sales and service specialists in ways that work for you...in person, on the phone, over the web

Service

- Guaranteed first-rate customer care from banking team, branch, telephone or internet
- Convenient, anytime access; it's easy to do business with us.
- We regularly ask for our customers' feedback and measure the results

Ideas

- Understanding your business is our number-one priority. We ask... and we listen
- Proactive, thoughtful ideas to help you grow your business, retain your employees, and accumulate wealth

Creating A Viable Go-To-Market Strategy

The sales culture at many banks promotes a *product pusher* mentality that leads to the existence of a large number of single-service customers. This is due in large part to existing incentive plans, or the product of the week that management wants to see succeed at all costs. Many business banking relationship managers find themselves too often leading with credit, for that has forever been their domain.

But in today's competitive marketplace, the needs of the typical business owner are ever changing and much more diverse. The following chart outlines the continuum of the business cycle and clearly shows the myriad of directions to which a typical business owner is being pulled on a daily basis:

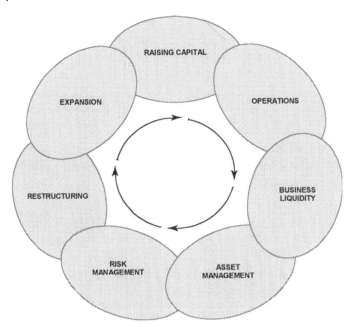

CONTINUUM OF THE BUSINESS LIFE CYCLE

Now, let's take one of these phases, such as raising capital, and look at its component parts—in short, all the areas where banks can provide products and services.

Raising Capital

- Small-business lease
- Small-business capital
- Letters of credit
- Traditional lending
- Tax-free and taxable-bond financing
- Construction lending
- Small-Business Administration (SBA) loans
- Commercial credit cards

This clearly reinforces the dangers inherent in leading with the single product, or credit, discussion. In those instances, a prospect or customer may not necessarily need a loan but may need help in some other areas. The prospect or customer may not necessarily offer up that information.

Bank marketers should instead be focusing on relationship, or *solution selling*, strategies that revolve around a total capital acquisition plan. That's an important first step in becoming a trusted financial advisor to your most important, and profitable, customers.

Instead of having a cash management discussion with a customer or prospect, speak in terms of helping them to maximize and leverage their total cash flow management structure. Or consult with them on growing and preserving wealth.

A major bank survey of their commercial customers revealed that a small business owner's number one concern in the near term was attracting and retaining their *own* employees. When a small business loses a key employee it can be devastating. It's like a football team losing their star quarterback.

As a bank, you have many products and services geared toward helping your customers attract and retain employees including banking-at-work programs, 401(k) plans, insurance, employee benefits and so forth. You need to package these and other products in coherent and relevant ways so that customers and prospects can easily see the strategic benefits of a long-term relationship with your bank.

Creating A Sustainable Competitive Advantage

Warren Buffett was once asked what is the most important thing he looks for when evaluating a company. Without hesitation, he replied, "sustainable competitive advantage."

Having the best product or service does not automatically guarantee you success. That's because:
- People do business with people they know
- People do business with people who do business with them
- People do business with people their friends talk about
- People do business with people they read about

Look at these four points to determine which area represents the greatest opportunity for your bank to gain an *unfair advantage*. An unfair advantage is doing something particularly well and better than your competition. And most importantly, it's an advantage that is sustainable through all types of internal change and market conditions.

And regardless of your bank's longevity in the marketplace, in today's competitive world you need to do everything a little bit better than you did yesterday.

Another necessary step in the process is determining the strategic focus of your bank. Are you operationally focused, product innovators or customer intimate? Take a look at the following descriptions for help in making that determination.

- **Operationally Focused**
  - These types of companies churn out products but have very little customer interaction at the purchase point. Examples of

these companies are consumer goods manufacturers such as Campbell's Soup, where products go from the plant to the distributor to the supermarket shelf. The only interaction with consumers occurs if there is a product defect, etc. A financial services example would be an Internet bank.

- **Product Innovators**
  - These types of companies create a new product and immediately move on to the next innovation. There is no customer interaction. Their customers want to talk about the present and they want to focus on the future. An example of this type of company would be Sony. Sony creates the next electronics innovation and moves on to the next. They don't have stores, they sell through retailers. They're not even sure who their customers are. That's why they ask so many questions on their warranty cards so they can create a customer demographic based on that information. It's the only way they know where to advertise.

- **Customer Intimate**
  - These are companies that provide products and services and boldly say, "I know your business almost as well as you do!" Wal-Mart is legendary for their customer information database and what they know about the buying habits of their customers. Banks that have achieved trusted advisor status with its customers fall into this category.

Hopefully your bank falls into the customer intimate category, which is the launching pad for developing a deep-set competitive advantage that can be sustained over time.

Putting On The Ritz

It's little wonder that the Ritz-Carlton Hotel is the only company to win the Malcolm Baldridge Quality Service Award *twice*! They have combined the utmost in quality service with an incomparable hotel experience that keeps customers coming back time after time.

Ritz-Carlton's Gold Standards are the foundation of the company. They encompass the values and philosophy by which they operate and include *The Credo, Three Steps of Service, 20 Basics, and The Employee Promise.*

The Credo

"The Ritz-Carlton Hotel is a place where the genuine care and comfort of our guests is our highest mission. We pledge to provide the finest personal service and facilities for our guests who will always enjoy a warm, relaxed, yet refined ambience. The Ritz-Carlton experience enlivens the senses, instills well-being, and fulfills even the unexpected wishes and needs of our guests."

Motto

"We are ladies and gentlemen serving ladies and gentlemen. This motto exemplifies the anticipatory service provided by all staff members."

Three Steps of Service

1. "A warm and sincere greeting. Use the guest's name, if and when possible."
2. "Anticipation and compliance with guest needs."
3. "Fond farewell. Give them a warm good-bye and use their names, if and when possible."

20 Basics

1. "The Credo is the principal belief of our Company. It must be known, owned and energized by all."
2. "Our Motto is: We are Ladies and Gentlemen serving Ladies and Gentlemen. As service professionals we treat our guests and each other with respect and dignity."
3. "The Three Steps of Service are the foundation of Ritz-Carlton hospitality. These steps must be used in every interaction to ensure satisfaction, retention and loyalty."
4. "The Employee Promise is the basis for our Ritz-Carlton work environment. It will be honored by all employees."
5. "All employees will successfully complete our annual Training Certification for their position."

6. "Company Objectives are communicated to all employees. It is everyone's responsibility to support them."
7. "To create pride and joy in the workplace, all employees have the right to be involved in the planning of the work that affects them."
8. "Each employee will continuously identify defects throughout the Hotel."
9. "It is the responsibility of each employee to create a work environment of teamwork and lateral service so that the needs of our guests and each other are met."
10. "Each employee is empowered. For example, when a guest has a problem or needs something special you should break away from your regular duties, address and resolve the issue."
11. "Uncompromising levels of cleanliness are the responsibility of every employee."
12. "To provide the finest personal service for our guests, each employee is responsible for identifying and recording individual guest preferences."
13. "Never lose a guest. Instant guest pacification is the responsibility of each employee. Whoever receives a complaint will own it, resolve it to the guest's satisfaction and record it."
14. "Smile—we are on stage. Always maintain positive eye contact. Use the proper vocabulary with our guests. (Use words like— Good Morning, Certainly, I'll be happy to, and My pleasure)."
15. "Be an ambassador of your Hotel in and outside of the work place. Always talk positively. Communicate any concerns to the appropriate person."
16. "Escort guests rather than pointing out directions to another area of the Hotel."
17. "Use Ritz-Carlton telephone etiquette. Answer within three rings and with a smile. Use the guest's name when possible."
18. "Take pride in and care of your personal appearance. Everyone is responsible for conveying a professional image by adhering to Ritz-Carlton clothing and grooming standards."
19. "Think safety first. Each employee is responsible for creating a safe, secure and accident-free environment for all guests and each other. Be aware of all fire and safety emergency procedures and report security risks immediately."

20. "Protecting the assets of a Ritz-Carlton is the responsibility of every employee. Conserve energy, properly maintain our hotels and protect the environment."

The Employee Promise

"At the Ritz-Carlton, our Ladies and Gentlemen are the most important resource in our service commitment to our guests. By applying the principles of trust, honesty, respect, integrity and commitment, we nurture and maximize talent to the benefit of each individual and company. The Ritz-Carlton fosters a work environment where diversity is valued, quality of life is enhanced, individual aspirations are fulfilled, and the Ritz-Carlton mystique is strengthened."

People who frequently stay at Ritz-Carlton hotels generally have a story or two about the legendary customer service. One of our favorites is the person who discovered that the water pressure in the shower was not up to their standards. They mentioned this fact as they checked out.

A number of months later this customer was checking into the same Ritz-Carlton Hotel when they were handed a personal note from the General Manager informing the guest that he himself had checked the water pressure in the guest's assigned room to ensure that it was up to the hotel's excellence standards. That's just one example of why people will drive by other four- and five-star hotels to stay at a Ritz-Carlton.

Surely there are many Ritz-Carlton principles that you could easily employ at your bank to create a more customer-friendly experience where employees are empowered to serve every need of the customer.

A True Quality Service Bank

Los Alamos National Bank (www.lanb.com), a community bank headquartered in Los Alamos, New Mexico, is the only bank in the United States to win the Malcolm Baldridge award. When you look closely at this bank you can see some striking similarities to the Ritz-Carlton model.

Like the Ritz-Carlton, Los Alamos hires employees based on attitude above everything else. They believe that it is far easier to teach someone the fundamentals of banking than it is to teach them about having the right attitude necessary to fit their unique corporate culture. As a result, many of their employees have never worked in banking before.

And every employee at Los Alamos is empowered to fix problems up to a certain dollar amount without the approval of a supervisor. Each year a certain amount of money is set aside for problem-resolution adjustments. Any money left over in the fund at year's end is equally distributed to all employees as a bonus. This encourages fixing the problem rather than merely throwing money at it.

Their brand promise is built on this solid foundation of quality customer service that has become part of the fabric of every employee and every transaction. The customer experience at Los Alamos is the same regardless of which branch a customer visits or which employee assists that customer.

The Dangers Of Pricing Strategies

As we begin to look at how many banks throughout the world are striving to create competitive advantages, let's first explore the disadvantages of using pricing as a long-term competitive advantage.

As the old adage goes, unless you're the lead dog on a dogsled team, than the scenery never changes. The three most critical pitfalls for using pricing as a competitive advantage are:

1. *Companies that compete solely on price do not create barriers to exit for their customers.* For banks, it leads to an excess of transactional customers who may have been attracted by a special savings rate and will only stay until the next best rate comes along. Those customers have not been given a compelling reason to stay. Retention is extremely important because studies have shown that it costs between five and six times more to attract a new customer than to keep an existing one. Just a 5% improvement in customer retention improves profitability from 25% to 100% according to Bain & Company. A major bank study on customer attrition rates over a one-year period revealed that while their quarterly attrition rate for customers with one product was 4.5%, that number dropped to 1.1% for customers with two products, and virtually to 0% for customers with

three or more products. So you can see that relationship selling not only reduces attrition rates, it can lead to the creation of satisfied customers. And that is the critical first step to creating customer advocates that will be most willing to tell your story to their family, friends and acquaintances.

2. *In service industries, discounted pricing often lead to discounted services in the customer relationship.* This is plain economics. When you reduce pricing without reducing costs you also reduce profits. When that happens, management is faced with lowering costs. And this often results in staff reductions, deteriorating customer service and the loss of other customer benefits.

3. *Pricing is less a true benefit than a perceived benefit when it is offered in the absence of long-term consultative or value-added services.* If the banker isn't providing strategic, value-added financial advice to business and personal customers, then these transactional customers will eventually migrate to other banks as those critical needs arise.

Value-Added Consultative Services

Many progressive banks throughout the world have developed keen insights into offering practical advice, professional help and cutting-edge ideas to both customers and prospects alike as a point of differentiation in the marketplace.

The Bank of Ireland (www.boi.ie) has developed a *Business Start-Up Package* consisting of a comprehensive bundle of internal products and services, external discounted offers, and educational support designed for new entrepreneurs.

Their product positioning is simple: "if you're thinking about starting your own business, we can offer help and expertise in more areas than you think, ensuring that you get the most out of the opportunities ahead."

The customers benefit from reduced start-up costs, customized solutions and additional support through external networks. The bank increases its share of wallet and customer retention, and encourages customer loyalty and advocacy through support of the business in the early, riskier years.

The Bank of Ireland also offers an in-house speakers bureau that enlists the collective talents of its staff and makes them available for group meetings either at the bank or at a customer location. Topics include employee benefit plans, managing cash flow, strategic and marketing planning, finances and investments for women, planning for retirement and a college-planning guide.

Bay Banks of Virginia (www.baybanks.com), and it's Bank of Lancaster, is another example of a bank that utilizes its in-house knowledge base to help their customers further grow and prosper.

This bank is also a cornerstone of their community and believes that the more successful the community, the more successful the bank. In fact, employees are expected to pay their *civic* rent through any number of community activity opportunities. This community involvement is part of every employee's annual performance review.

Farm Credit Canada (www.fcc-fac.ca) offers specialized industry services in their predominantly agricultural portfolio. These services include a range of agricultural-related software programs geared to increase farm productivity and field and crop management. In addition, the bank also offers a special accounting and cash management software tool, a team of advisors with agricultural backgrounds and an annual subscription to a weekly agricultural news bulletin.

This helps position Farm Credit as the agricultural banking expert in the field and, like Bank of Ireland, helps to increase revenue and promote the type of loyalty that results in a wealth of referrals from satisfied customers.

Now let's take a look at how some banks are differentiating themselves through a variety of strategies such as customer experience, convenience, product innovation and superior customer service.

Customer Experience Differentiator

There has been an explosion in recent years by banks to overhaul the appearance of their branches in order to create a more pleasant *shopping* experience, borrowing heavily from the retail industry.

As we mentioned earlier, *Umpqua Bank* has been an early banking pioneer in the customer experience phenomenon. In a 2007 interview with *Banking Strategies* magazine, their President and CEO Ray Davis said: "I have to say that all of the things that we've done are not necessarily rocket science. They are basic marketing and management strategies. I don't think we've necessarily come up with a new idea; however, we have borrowed ideas from a variety of industries."

"The big question that I asked myself when I first came to Oregon 12 years ago was: How do you differentiate a bank? We were as good as any other bank in the market. We quickly determined that it made no sense for us to try to differentiate ourselves with more resources, technology or advertising because the big banks had more than we did. And, we felt it made no sense to try to differentiate ourselves with bank products because they truly are a commodity."

"So, how do you differentiate banking? We were focused on two things. One was the delivery system; we felt the way you deliver products could be unique. Two, you can create an incredible customer experience. For us, we were clear very early on that it was about brand creation and building a reputation for service. To do this, we really focused on creating our unique customer experience through a measurable customer service program."

And deliver they did. Their customers are referred to as guests. They try to offer their guests a sensory experience when they come into the branch (which they refer to as stores). They have created a fun, comfortable atmosphere and offer customers a positive banking encounter. The bank was among the first to establish a cyber café and to sell its own brand of coffee and T-shirts. Many customers come in at all times of the day to watch CNN on the large screen TV, read Forbes or the Wall Street Journal, check email, surf the web on any number of laptop computers, or just to mingle with other customers and non-customers over a cup of Umpqua's own unique blend of coffee.

But branch transformation is not just for the larger asset banks. *Union National Community Bank* (www.uncb.com) is a small community bank headquartered in Lancaster, Pennsylvania, with about $300 million in assets and a handful of branches.

A couple of years ago they created the *Gold Cafe* which they describe as simply the newest, most outwardly visible form of the reinvigorated corporate culture within the overall Union National Community Bank brand. And the name of the bank doesn't appear anywhere on the Gold Cafe building.

Every team member of Gold Cafe is trained as a *financial barista*. In other words, not only has each team member had highly skilled training in financial services and the overall customer experience, but each has also had significant training in the art of serving the perfect cup of coffee.

Gold Cafe is far from a traditional banking environment. The walls are painted with bold colors—red, yellow, green and blue. They've exposed the ceilings, the brick, and the concrete floors, and the coffee bar is textural with its inclusion of corrugated aluminum.

Several plasma screens also hang overhead with a range of customized video content and the space even offers free WiFi access and a patio that features outdoor seating.

Cornerstone Bank (www.cornerstonebankga.com), a community bank in Atlanta, opened a new branch that quickly became an extension of their brand. The branch is complete with red branding walls, custom merchandizing pieces that incorporate the bank's logo, digital media on a custom plasma screen, a coffee station and comfortable seating areas.

We have also seen evidence of this phenomenon during our trips to the Middle East to conduct bank-marketing seminars. For instance, the *National Bank of Kuwait* (www.nbk.com) has created *Thahabi* lounges—dedicated, private lounges for their top tier customers. And the *Arab Bank* (www.arabbank.com) underwent a massive branch-remodeling project that contains many of the same innovations found at Umpqua or Washington Mutual branches.

Customer Convenience Differentiator

Clearly, the trendsetter in this category would have to be *Commerce Bank* (www.commerceonline.com), headquartered in Cherry Hill, New Jersey. They refer to themselves simply as *America's Most Convenient Bank*.

Commerce, which was acquired by Toronto-Dominion Bank in late 2007, decided at its founding that it would compete solely on the promise of being the most convenient bank for customers. Their branches are open seven days a week and the bank considers its employees to be retailers and not bankers. Commerce also employs many of the same service principles of the fast-food restaurant industry where its founder was a major franchisee.

Commerce credits a simple set of basic strategies for its success:
- Know your position. If your bank stands for *convenience*, ensure that convenience comes through in every decision you make.
- Look to your best-in-class retail neighbors for ideas. What are their hours? How are their associates dressed? How are they bringing their brand to life?
- Consistency in customer experience: Make it easy for your customers, the less they have to think about where the teller line is, the more they'll think about your latest promotion
- *No stupid rules!* Everyone should embrace the rule of never making a policy that your most entry-level staff member can't understand and communicate.
- Make sure you know what is really happening. You must consistently shop and measure in order to ensure that your strategy is really being executed.

Commerce believes that every great retailer has a differentiated model and that products alone cannot be the basis for differentiation. The Commerce model focuses on convenience, friendly people and *no* stupid rules.

Product Innovation Differentiator

CEOs across all industries cite product innovation as one of the most valuable means of meeting customer demand and aiding organic growth. Financial services institutions must take solutions that exist today and make them easier to use or more widely applicable to their customers.

The ascent of the reinvented product enables institutions to effectively differentiate their offerings in a period of rising growth expectations, strained margins and increased competition.

Some of the world's most successful companies have fostered an innovation culture that enables them to remain on the cutting edge of product development and customer experience.

The *3M Company* has a strong internal culture of creativity that results in a high success rate in turning ideas in health care, industrial components and other areas into profitable products that consumers want.

Apple uses outstanding design and a steady flow of ideas from employees to redefine old categories such as their iPod.

Proctor & Gamble can trace its product innovation to a continuous dedication to understanding changing consumer lifestyles.

And *Starbucks* reframed the coffee business as a lifestyle brand by watching customers and then creating a strong consumer affinity to the brand that helps them to sell new products, such as music CDs.

Bank of America's (www.bankofamerica.com) *Keep the Change*™ program is a great example of an innovative way to cross-sell savings accounts to checking customers, and to boost the balances of existing savings accounts.

Each time a *Bank of America* customer buys something with their Bank of America Visa® debit card, the bank will round up their purchase to the nearest dollar amount and transfer the difference from their checking account to their savings account. Customers get to keep the change and grow their savings.

For small business customers, Bank of America offers an online business resource called *Business 24/7*™ that is positioned to provide a broader range of capabilities to improve money management processes for time-constrained small business owners. Customers can integrate all of their accounts—including those from other banks—onto a single dashboard. Customers can create their own invoices and set email alerts for things like payment reminders, past due notices and payment notifications.

Charlotte, NC, rival *Wachovia Bank* (www.wachovia.com) launched its own innovative savings product named *Way2Save*SM *Automatic Savings Account.* Way2Save transfers $1 from the customer's checking account to a high-yield savings account every time a customer makes a purchase with their Check Card or makes an electronic payment.

USAA (www.USAA.com) has made remote check deposit a snap for consumers from the comfort of their homes. *The USAA Deposit@ Home*™ is a free service that enables customers to deposit checks from home if they have a computer with a Windows 2000 or XP operating system with Internet Explorer 5.0 or higher and a scanner with a resolution of at least 200 dots per inch.

To capitalize on a growing youth market in India, *Icici Bank's* (www.icicibank.com) *Young Stars* program combines financial education with free banking products such as checkbooks, free debit cards and free Internet banking for children up to 18 years old.

Young Stars also offers savings and investment options to the parents, along with aids to help teach their children to manage their personal finances in a more responsible and independent manner. Indications from Icici Bank are that many of these young customers are staying with the bank long after their nineteenth birthday.

As the world becomes more environmentally conscious, many banks have turned to green initiatives to create goodwill in their communities and a point of differentiation in the marketplace.

Alpine Bank of Colorado (www.alpinebank.com) has created the *Alpine Bank Green Team* that injects a strong sense of social responsibility into everything that they do. The grass-roots employee *Green Team* helps the bank to understand and measure their energy and water consumption and waste production.

And Alpine Bank gets customers actively engaged in their green program by suggesting ways to save time and protect against fraud, including:
- Signing up for electronic banking statements for checking and other deposit accounts.
- Signing up for direct deposit of paychecks, retirement checks or Social Security benefits.
- Having regular bills such as telephone or credit cards sent via Online BillPay and then paying the bills online.
- Using Online Banking, ATMs or automated voice service to check account balances.
- Using automated debits to pay bills that are the same amount each month.

Quality Service Differentiator

While Los Alamos National Bank is in a league of its own from a quality service perspective, many banks such as *Bank of Smithtown* (www.bankofsmithtownonline.com) are differentiating themselves in the marketplace through their exceptional customer service.

Headquartered in Long Island, New York, Bank of Smithtown employees are rewarded for questioning bank practices that are not deemed to be in the best interest of the customer or the bank. Their philosophy is that if what you're selling isn't in the best interests of the customer, then you'll never gain the customer's trust. The bank firmly believes that service is not a commodity, but a differentiating factor.

Branch personnel are called Bank Pros™ because they have been cross-trained to handle all the bank's services. Specialized transactions that require an expert are referred on the spot. Regardless of the customer need, all efforts are geared toward the customer getting an answer before they leave the branch. Totally remodeled branches, together with Bank Pros, have generated excitement and a great brand in the marketplace.

Chapter Keys:

1. Create a meaningful value proposition that is in the best interest of your customers
2. Develop a go-to-market strategy that resonates with each market segment
3. Identify what your bank does best and see if you can turn it into a sustainable competitive advantage

CHAPTER 14

Creating A Circle of Trust With Customers

It seems like you can't pick up a magazine, watch television or surf the Internet today without being inundated with messages from banks and non-banks all vying to be your trusted financial advisors. And they're all promising to treat you as a most important individual.

But the reason for the proliferation of this type of advertising is the fact that today's consumers and business owners not only demand this type of treatment, they *expect* it.

We mentioned in an earlier chapter that in complex intangible service businesses, such as banking, *trust* is more important than differentiation. Buyers of complex intangible services are buying specialized expertise. They are seeking an expert because they don't want to, or can't be, an expert in the service they are buying. Given a choice, they prefer to find a qualified expert they trust, rather than evaluate the expertise of many different alternatives.

We also mentioned the importance that trust has in creating loyal retail and business customer advocates who are willing to refer family, friends and business associates. And the key to gaining that trust depends upon the ability of bankers to forge strategic partnerships with customers by becoming trusted financial advisors.

For example, many of today's Fortune 500 companies can trace their humble beginnings back to an entrepreneur with a vision. Apple Computer began in a garage in California with two young men— Steve Jobs and Steve Wosniak—and a sketch on a paper napkin. In partnership with venture capitalists—and later bankers—that shared that vision, we now know that that sketch became the Macintosh Computer and the rest is history. But in today's banking world, this has become more the exception than the rule.

Without having the intimate knowledge of a customer's vision, and the future potential of a product or service, your bank may be missing opportunities to grow along with high potential companies.

True, you may never run into a potential Apple Computer as a customer. But how many potential profitable relationships is your bank missing because they don't have a clue what their customers do for a living, or what kind of upside their products might have in the near future?

More and more, consumers are turning to non-banking financial advisors because of the trust that those companies have earned over time. On the commercial side, business owners are turning to their accountants and attorneys when making critical business decisions. That's because banks do not share the same status that accountants and attorneys do in the eyes of customers when it comes to business advisory decisions.

In fact, a major bank study by the Business Banking Board revealed that when seeking advice for cash management services, business customers chose their accountants over their bankers by a margin of 53% to 14% as illustrated in the following chart.

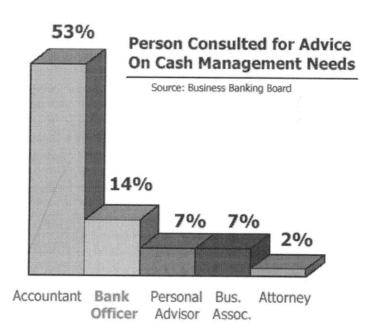

Person Consulted for Advice On Cash Management Needs

Source: Business Banking Board

53% — Accountant
14% — Bank Officer
7% — Personal Advisor
7% — Bus. Assoc.
2% — Attorney

And there is an inherent danger when accountants and attorneys recommend a financial institution to one of their customers. They may very well be recommending one of your bank's customers to a competitor.

Because the industry is mature and competitive, institutions must differentiate themselves to boost their customer acquisition rates. The most common strategy for becoming more compelling to targeted prospects involves an ambition to serve as a trusted advisor.

At the very least, this is definitely something that your bank should be offering to their most profitable customers who are critical to the long-term success of the bank.

Indeed, when business customers are asked why they continue to turn to non-bank advisors for financial advice they stated that bank relationship managers spend most of their time on non-advice related activities surrounding traditional financial products such as loans and lines of credit. This has caused an atmosphere where financial services providers wonder how they can become more relevant to customers and prospects alike.

For the trusted advisor, differentiation is much less connected to brand image. In a nutshell, branding can get you on the short list, but differentiation gets you the sale—and differentiation is very much about the individual's experience of the sales and advisory process.

Absent this partnership, customers will view low cost as the only value delivered by their banking services provider. We mentioned in an earlier chapter that pricing is less a true benefit than a perceived benefit when it is offered in the absence of long-term consultative or value-added services.

The first step in attempting to create a trusted advisor strategy throughout the bank is to first determine the business strategy that your bank will pursue going forward. There are three distinct business strategies when looking at most banks:

- *Low-Cost:*
  - Least cost and most efficient operating structure in delivering a specific product set; uses price as a competitive weapon to win customer market share.

- *Customer-Centric:*
  - Customers are the key asset and driver in defining business requirements, including product design and service delivery.

- *Innovative:*
  - Agile organization structure that fosters constant monitoring of customers and competition, and rapid and creative responses to changes.

Banks that describe their primary business strategy as being **innovative** had better financial performance than other banks according to a research report entitled, "Customer Metrics Survey: A Quantitative Analysis of Effective Customer Strategies," by Financial Insights in Framingham, MA.

The study examined the connection between business performance measurement, the use of customer metrics, and how the metrics were being used to create better results. The results showed that banks following the innovative strategy were by far the highest performers and faced fewer obstacles when applying and using customer metrics.

The obstacles to this strategy were identified as problems in such areas as data gathering, measuring and quality, organizational skills and costs, single view of the customer, Return On Investment (ROI) metrics, organizational support, and technology support and costs.

The study also stated that innovative companies have a more common understanding of who the customer is, and what will drive additional value to that customer and to the bank. So it's not a question of who owns the customer, but rather the ways in which banks can add value to the relationship.

People will not listen to people that they cannot *connect* with at some level. A Harvard University study found that for people to want to do business with you they must feel a connection first—they must trust you. And the more we speak to successful people, the more they credit their success to the ability to turn business acquaintances into trusted partners and friends.

And this partnering is very important, especially when it creates customer advocates most willing to refer potential customers to a bank. Research has shown that customer conversion rates from third-party referral sources close at a rate *two-and-one-half* times that of traditional prospecting methods. This suggests that friends of the bank have much more sway with prospects than the bank does itself.

Starting A Trusted Advisor Program

A key strategy to achieve organic growth objectives should be to selectively convert some of your retail and business salespeople into trusted advisors. This partnership with the customer will ultimately lead to greater value to both the personal *and* business goals of customers, while helping the bank's bottom line for years to come.

As we said earlier, financial institutions are still too focused on single product sales instead of on the broader solutions to customer needs. Consumers do not buy products based solely upon advertised benefits. People buy a product or service only because they believe it will solve certain problems and give them certain results.

People buy a hammer at the hardware store because it is an integral component to an important project. The bottom line is that the hammer must solve a problem and deliver results in order for the overall project to be considered a success.

Once someone has decided that they have a problem that they need solved, then they will make a conscious decision as to who will solve it for them. If you have focused the conversation on telling them all about how and what your service is, they will feel that you are too focused on yourself and your needs. When the focus is on you, people get the sense that you have your own best interest at heart and don't really care about them.

An organization is truly innovative in its approach to being a trusted financial advisor when it properly manages information, makes that information available to the right people, and trains its staff to use that to build relationship value.

Many banks will argue that existing compensation and incentive programs impede their efforts in implementing the quick changes necessary to put their bankers on the road to providing the type of financial advice that is entirely in the best interest of the customer.

But any time that you help a customer to grow their business it stands to reason that the need for additional financial products and services will continue to grow providing added revenue to the bank, and additional compensation to the banker, in the long term.

First and foremost, a trusted advisor strategy is about influencing the right behaviors necessary to deliver the right solutions for each customer. You can't be expected to completely overhaul your compensation and incentive programs every time you make a change to your sales process and strategy. You need to roll it out slowly and be able to offer incremental incentives as the program merits.

The five-step process outlined in the following chart can be used in two ways. First, as an interim process to influence certain sales behaviors. Then the process can be implemented in stages over a period of time until you get to the point where the new sales strategy becomes part of the corporate culture. You can then tie the sales person's compensation directly to the long-term goals of the bank.

Compensation Plans That Support Cross-Sales

Compensation Type	Description	Advantages
Bonus Points Towards an Existing Compensation Plan	Relationship managers are rewarded for qualified referrals with bonus points towards performance targets	Bonus point systems links cross-sales and compensation while minimizing disruption to existing incentive plan
Referral-Based Cash Bonuses	Bank provides cash bonuses to RMs for qualified referrals	Immediate, tangible incentive; cash bonuses are easy to manage
Incentives for Achievement Of Cross-Sell Targets	Bank establishes cross-sell targets for RMs and ties a percentage of compensation to performance against those targets	Allows Bank to set clear cross-sell performance goals and to hold RMs accountable for those targets
Bank Performance Based Incentives	Bank ties a percentage of RM compensation to overall organizational performance	RMs are invested in the overall profitability of the organization
Graduated Payouts	Bank provides RMs with graduated payouts based on customer profitability over time	Long-term goals encourage RMs to cross-sell valuable products that meet customer needs & build relationships

Step One: Customer Listening

Every so often, bankers need to stop and ponder what's it like to be _our customer_. By combining the insights of both the customer and the bank on an ongoing basis, you can ensure that you are always asking the right questions in order to provide solutions to all the financial needs and concerns of your customers.

We know exactly what it's like to be a customer. Insurance companies, the department store, the auto dealership. Some experiences are better than others. We know the things that we don't like and won't tolerate. Sometimes we complain about a bad experience and sometimes we choose to move on. And when we're gone there's no turning back. We appreciate a value proposition and things like good customer service, a fair price and promises that are kept. Those are some of the things that build loyalty and trust and keep us coming back time and time again.

But too often bankers cease to *think* like customers. Now, more than ever, in this intensely competitive environment, you should always be asking yourselves, what's it like to be *our* customer?

What your customers are thinking, and what you think is on their minds are often times two different things. Before you make a phone call to a customer or attend a customer meeting, take a moment to ponder the following questions:

- *Is it easy to do business with us?*
  Do your products work as well as you think? Is your customer service above average? If it's not the customer will leave at some point. In short, does your bank make it easy to do business with them?

- *How do they perceive your customer service?*
  The banker may be doing a great job, but the bank may be making errors that are irritating the customer. But they may not mention that to the banker because they either think that the problem is outside of the banker's sphere of responsibility or that the banker simply doesn't care about the problem.

- *Are you taking care of their business <u>and</u> personal needs?*
  How can you be perceived as a trusted financial advisor if you never ask a business customer about their personal needs? That's why many banks have an enormous number of single-service business customers. If you never ask a business customer about their personal needs how can that customer perceive that you are interested in everything about them?

- *Are you suggesting better or more innovative ways to meet their present and future needs?*
  Are you taking the time to get to know your customer's future goals and aspirations so you can provide the correct course of action regarding their financial options? Remember, if the customer grows their business then there's a better than average chance that the customer will provide more profitability to the bank.

- *Are you asking the right questions in order to uncover their concerns?*
  Many customers will not volunteer information without being asked. You may not be aware of a problem until that customer has left the bank.

- *If concern areas are outside your scope of responsibility are you alerting the appropriate people so problems can be addressed and corrected?*
  Even if a customer concern is outside of your scope of responsibility it is incumbent upon you to help to get it fixed and then close the information loop by advising your customer of the outcome.

- *Are you achieving a value proposition?*
  Are you viewed as a product pusher or as someone who the customer perceives as adding value to their relationship with the bank?

- *Are you employing all of the Bank's resources for the benefit of the customer?*
  Do you work to gather the collective resources of the bank to help your customer grow and prosper?

Step Two: Getting To Know Your Customers And Prospects

It is inconceivable that in today's marketplace there are banks that do business with retail and business customers without knowing what makes them tick. How can you possibly provide long-term value to a small business without knowing anything about what that company does day in and day out? Or how can you help a couple with their long-term financial planning without knowing their ultimate goals and objective?

The greatest CRM or MCIF in the world won't provide you with the whole story unless there is a concerted effort to add very personal information to each customer profile.

For retail customers, a bank marketing colleague of ours has customized their CRM system to create *Customer Interest* screens. Through their interactions with customers or prospects, they glean important personal information from them, such as:

- Their Birthday
- Spouse's name
- Children's names and ages
- Favorite College team
- College alma mater

They use that information to connect with their customers and prospects. For example, every customer gets a birthday card personally signed by the bank president.

The best way to have a *meaningful* conversation with a customer or prospect is to have an intimate knowledge of how each customer makes their money. It's not just enough anymore to know that a small business is a plastics manufacturer.

What are the short- and long-term outlooks for the plastics industry? Do you know how that customer's products are used in other applications? What is the economic outlook for the raw materials essential to your customer's business?

You don't need a crystal ball to figure this out or spend hours surfing the Internet. There are a number of companies that provide industry research and company reports containing a wealth of information on particular industries, economic outlooks and performance of companies within given industries.

Step Three: Setting Up The Calling Program

I'm sure you'll agree that nothing good happens from a business perspective until you are sitting across the desk from a customer or prospect. The days of sitting in your office and dialing for dollars are long gone.

The first step in creating a trusted advisor program is to get relationship managers comfortable with making a set number of face-to-face calls with customers and prospects on a monthly basis. For the first few months this becomes a numbers game as bankers begin to master the habit of making those monthly calls. But that's the first step in influencing new behaviors that will be perceived as being in the best interest of the customer.

After a few months of these calling efforts, you can then begin to inspect the *quality* of conversations that the bankers are having with their customers. Sales Managers can then determine an appropriate frequency of contact that a banker should have with a given client based on their realistic needs.

Once the bankers are comfortable with the quantity and quality of their calling efforts, you can then begin the process of systematically profiling each customer to determine the business and personal needs and goals, as well as the profit potential, of each customer over a period of time.

Many banks have developed a comprehensive profile form that they expect the banker to complete for a set number of customers over a series of meetings. The first meeting might cover ownership interests, years in business, fixed assets and the like. Subsequent meetings would cover areas such as business succession planning—will the company be sold or passed on to family members—as well as growing and preserving wealth, capital acquisition strategy and maximizing and leveraging cash flow.

Not only does this create a level of comfort and good will with customers, it also takes the guesswork out of each banker's pipeline reports because now they will have a better understanding of the real needs of their customers.

A Trusted Advisor Profile:
ServisFirst Bank

Adapted from an article in Fortune Small Business,
March 7, 2008, by Patricia B. Gray

At first glance, ServisFirst Bank of Birmingham, Alabama, might look like your typical de novo bank started by an entrepreneur with a vision. But a closer look reveals that this bank has no tellers, no ATMs, no advertising, no teaser-rate CDs, no fancy offices and no lollipops in the lobby.

In fact, ServisFirst doesn't want their customers, or potential customers, to come and see them. The bankers prefer to visit the customer and prospect sites to see for themselves how these companies make their money.

And they must be doing something right. Since its founding in 2005, the bank has grown from $35 million in assets when it opened its doors to $850 million in assets at the end of 2007. It was named as one of the top ten fastest-growing banks in the United States according to a study by Donnelly Penman & Partners, an investment bank in Michigan.

ServisFirst has made this meteoric rise by maintaining its sharp focus on its core customer—busy small business owners who want fast, personal service and are willing to pay a premium for that attention.

The bank's founder, Tom Broughton, finds most banks pretty annoying. He thinks they require too much paperwork from customers and take too long to make a loan decision. And he doesn't understand why bankers don't spend more time on their customer's turf when they profess to be so concerned about the state of their businesses.

ServisFirst bankers have trekked through coal mines, construction sites, farm fields and factories in their quest for new business. They firmly believe that their intimate knowledge of a customer's business will enable them to make value judgments on a company's profit potential that wouldn't be apparent to another bank that just focuses on the company's financials.

"A good banker doesn't sit at his desk waiting for the computer to decide whether to make a loan," says Broughton. "Your banker should know your story, and he's the one who makes the case for your loan to me."

Step Four: Inspect What You Expect

Accountability is the key to any successful sales management program, and tracking methods can range from sophisticated company-wide intranet programs to basic, inexpensive software programs for smaller banks with fewer salespeople.

We've seen banks that track this information on index cards, on Excel spreadsheets or with inexpensive call management software programs.

Banks that have made these calling efforts part of the overall goal for each banker have seen a rise in both productivity and revenue. Accountability is the key to any successful sales management program, and the tracking of calling programs should be as important as the tracking of sales and revenue results.

Many banks have scorecards for their bankers that track sales and revenue products such as loans, deposits and cash management. Banks that actively track sales calling efforts include in their scorecards a monthly goal for business profiles completed as well as face-to-face meetings with customers and prospects.

Chapter Keys:

1. Become a trusted financial advisor to your key retail and business customers
2. Develop flexible compensation programs that promote cross-selling
3. Learn as much as possible about your business customers and their unique challenges to compete within that industry

CHAPTER 15

Keeping In Step With Your Customer And Market

"Moss doesn't grow on a rolling stone," provides an excellent parallel indicator to our next discussion of keeping up with your customers and market. Just as moss does not have time to adhere to a rolling stone, sometimes you have a hard time keeping up with the dynamic nature of your customers' lives.

However, you have to find ways to keep a pulse on your customers, your market and your relationship with both. As a financial marketer, you need to have a process and mechanism of keeping on the same page as your target market as it evolves and changes. But keeping tabs of your customers is both easy and difficult (don't you love life's little challenges?). The easy part is watching behavioral outcomes (closing accounts, opening accounts, adding balances, etc.). The difficult part is ascertaining what specifically is driving those actions.

There are many research methods you can employ to keep up-to-date information on your customers. They range from the internal collection of data and statistics to broad customer surveys and market analysis. Each plays a role in creating a true 360-degree understanding of the main stakeholders in your marketing equation including customers, staff and non-customers.

While most institutions gather information about their customers, fewer gather information from their staff or from non-customers. You can learn a tremendous amount from those that do not bank with your institution. Are they consciously choosing to not bank with you, do they have any awareness of your points of differentiation, or are their needs unmet by your products or services? Each offers a vastly different approach to the solution.

Common Internal Tools

- *Staff comment line-* a dedicated voice mail extension to allow staff to offer input, feedback, ideas or challenges
- *Usage statistics of delivery channels-* gathering of use data by various segments of your customer base, trend the data to identify growth or decline
- *Customer account opening/closing surveys-* a last chance gathering of feedback from a customer that is closing their account or what led them to their action
- *Staff exit interviews-* a last chance gathering of feedback from an employee that is leaving the institution on the climate of the organization and thoughts for improvement

Common External Tools

- *Telephone survey-* broad survey to determine a host of variable issues, usually with a statistically representative sample of your entire customer base
- *Branch intercept surveys-* geographic/location-based surveys that help to uncover strengths and weaknesses for a particular office
- *Email surveys-* a quick and easy method to reach out to customers for obtaining a quick pulse on a certain narrowly-defined issue
- *Website surveys-* specific questions to visitors of your website about functionality, usage, unmet functionality and needs, etc.
- *Unaided awareness studies-* help you to determine your market awareness levels by asking a respondent, without prompt or knowledge of the sponsor, to name the first three institutions that come to mind

The process you choose is probably more important than the individual method you use to collect the data. Each method has pros and cons for its value, ease of use and depth of information. However, the process will define the relevance of the information to the issue you need to resolve. As noted from Converge, Inc. the process is comprised of four key areas; plan, implement, analyze and act. Each is a critical step to ensure that the information you are gathering will be actionable for your organization.

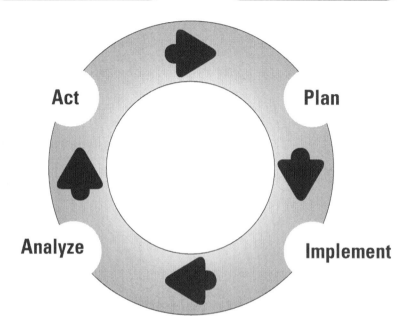

Act on the result of the surveys:

Feedback and reporting to employee

Reveiw the conclusions of the analysis

Develop action plans based upon interpretation of the data

Plan the survey:

Identify the basic areas of interest and research questions

Define the specific measures and metrics

Develop the specific question set

Design the basic analytical plan

Act

Plan

Analyze

Implement

Analyze the survey:

Analyze high level data for organizational wide patterns

Breakdown analysis on sub-groupings of data:
Departments
Geography

Time based analysis to highlight trends and patterns

Implement the survey:

Define the research frame and gather the sample

Distribute the questionaire:
Phone   Print
Web   E-mail

Manage completion process and response rates

Adapted from Converge, Inc.

Actionable customer research should enable your organization to align itself with the marketplace. Your marketplace is made up of a series of environments including economic, competitive, political and communication. Each component requires information, analysis, benchmarking and evaluation. A quick summary of the issues related to each marketplace environment:

Economic Environment
- Rate surveys
- Pricing surveys
- Fee surveys
- Business growth/retraction

Competitive Environment
- Competitive analysis and assessment
- Product niches
- New office locations or market expansion

Political Environment
- Political changes
- Regulation restrictions, new policies
- Market analysis – new construction, roads, businesses, etc.

Communication Environment
- Media changes
- Advertising volumes
- New media outlets

As with the customer research, it is important to truly understand your information needs and then apply research techniques to acquire appropriate information. You can acquire multiple information pieces concerning the marketplace from secondary sources, such as:
- FDIC.gov
- Census.gov
- Real estate firms
- County government agencies

The integration of information and research is the most fundamentally important aspect. You must turn the information received into actionable knowledge and strategy that leads to focused tactics.

Chapter Keys:

1. Gather information pertinent to support your marketing strategies
2. Follow a research process that culminates in the information refined and transformed into actionable strategy and analysis
3. Focus on both the customer information needs and the marketplace

CHAPTER 16

Make Your Website A Destination

Think Outside The Screen

Given the time constraints of today's very active consumers it comes as little surprise that a majority of people will migrate to the Internet first in search of information, product advice and feedback from peers.

Advertisers around the world are expected to double their spending on the Internet during the next three years as more people get their news and entertainment on the Web instead of television, radio, newspapers and magazines. The trend is expected to create an $80 billion online ad market in 2010, up from an estimated $40 billion last year.

As we mentioned earlier, people are not just interested in how your product or service works, but rather how it fits into their current lifestyle. Yet a scan of many banking websites reveals screen after screen of self-serving product information making it virtually impossible to differentiate the value of one bank over another.

And that is forcing consumers and business owners to go elsewhere to get unbiased advice on their most pressing concerns. Let's take a look at some web sites that are helping consumers with basic financial decision-making.

- *CNN Money Budget Calculator*
  - Consumers can input things like your salary and tax information, and it'll suggest what they can afford for housing, insurance, and other big-ticket categories, plus it helps them divide up what's left for leisure activities.

- *Bankrate.com Debt Pay-Down Adviser*
  - This will help consumers to figure out how quickly they'll whittle down their credit card balances if they increase their monthly payments. Once they've seen what a big difference a few extra dollars a month will make they might be more inclined to alter their budget to pay more each month.

- **_The SmartMoney "How Long Will My Money Last?" Calculator_**
  - Retirees can learn how much money their current retirement investments will generate annually in their leisure years. If it looks like they might not have enough saved yet to live the type of life they desire, they can then simply follow the link to retirement-strategy worksheets to see how to increase their bottom line.

- **_MSN Money Central College Savings Calculator_**
  - How much will students have to save to afford college? Or what's their tuition limit based on their current savings rate? It's not too soon to think about these questions—and do something. There's useful financial information as well on how to invest wisely and protect their financial privacy.

What each of these web sites has in common is that they are offering advice on issues of critical concerns to consumers. And this advice has nothing to do with the _product_ that they sell (although the advertisers on those sites will be happy to sell you the products necessary to achieve your goals). These web sites are adding value to each site visitor who is all too happy to refer it to family and friends.

There is absolutely nothing in these four examples that a bank couldn't host on their web site as a value-added service geared to helping consumers to get more educated around financial issues.

The typical bank advertising or direct mail campaign designed to sell a home mortgage or home equity loan resonates mostly with an audience that is _already_ in the market for some sort of home renovation project or other high-ticket purchase. But these marketing programs tend to ignore that portion of the market that can be motivated or influenced to _start_ thinking about it.

It would be relatively simple to set up a home improvement resource on a bank web site geared to helping consumers through the home improvement process, such as offering financial calculators, tips on selecting an architect and a contractor, and other relevant information.

A bank could even enlist some of their customers who are in the home remodeling business to contribute articles and design ideas for home renovation. If you help to educate the consumer they will be more inclined to come to you for the products to make it all happen.

Banks should ask themselves what they would do differently if they were trying to attract advertisers to their web site depending solely on how many site visits the bank generated. In that case, you can bet that many banks would start to take a much more financial advisory approach to their web sites and position their products and services in a more value-added light.

Some Banks Are Capitalizing On The Social Networking Craze

Social networking happens before business, and not vice versa. And many popular social networking web sites such as YouTube, Facebook and MySpace have captured the attention of some very prominent banks such as JPMorgan Chase, ING Direct and Wells Fargo.

Banks have discovered that these sites offer an attractive venue for promoting their products and services. Social networks have grown exponentially in recent years. YouTube draws over 20 million unique visitors per month and adds more than 65,000 videos per day.

Chase uses Facebook, a virtual campus of five million students, to promote its credit card for college students. Facebook users can earn *Karma Points* by making purchases at certain stores and even getting friends to sign up for a Chase credit card. They can accumulate these points, give them away, or redeem them for cool rewards from Chase.

In an effort to generate more interest in its mortgage products, ING launched a web site called *MoveOutMoveUp.com*, which targets first-time homebuyers with humorous video clips and games. The video clips have circulated the Internet and been featured on YouTube, gaining more exposure for ING's products.

More than 40% of ING's business comes from referrals, and being featured on a third-party web site has the perception of an independent endorsement.

Wells Fargo has launched a number of blogs in an effort to more fully engage online customers. The first, *Guided By History*, was started in conjunction with the 100th anniversary of the 1906 earthquake that leveled the bank's headquarters city of San Francisco. It contains personal accounts from the earthquake, historical anecdotes and information about how families can prepare for disasters.

Wells Fargo has another blog called *StudentLoanDown* that includes first-person stories on student loan experiences, information about tuition rates and financial aid, and other advice and resources relevant to students.

The Internet has also spawned a host of web sites and blogs where like-minded people can network to gain valuable insights and ideas to improve their marketing programs or enhance their careers. For instance, the American Bankers Association's Marketing Network has a special ListServ for members that allows bankers to communicate with their marketing peers throughout the United States.

Chapter Keys:

1. In addition to product information, offer practical financial advice on your web site
2. Include useful links on your web site that provides visitors with information that is pertinent to their lifestyles
3. Constantly explore opportunities to have your bank participate on social networking web sites in an appropriate manner

CHAPTER 17

Making Fundamental Process Changes

"We are what we repeatedly do. Excellence then, is not an act, but a habit."

- Aristotle

Once you have studied, analyzed and realized the environmental shifts of the industry, you may need to make fundamental process changes in important areas. Consistent application, evaluation and implementation will drive the development of the entire process into daily action and expectation. Being the agent of change within your organization requires your knowledge of the global changes, the regional changes, and how each applies to your institution. Three key areas of fundamental process change that will, undoubtedly, drive your efforts are:

1. Internal culture and your experience
2. How you do business
3. Managing change

Internal culture and your experience

The internal culture, as we have described and outlined it, needs to be defined and refined as it relates to the goals, brand promise and organizational strengths of an organization.

Development of engagement across the organization, both vertically and horizontally, is mission critical to the adoption and integration of the industry shifts. Vertical engagement ensures that from the board level down to the customer contact level that marketing is ever present, that employees are involved and feel engaged, and that the institution provides opportunity for them personally and professionally. Horizontal engagement means that all areas across the bank are involved, and that you include all customer areas and product delivery channels.

Your customer experience, combined with the staff experience and culture, delivers an environment that creates and builds growth and opportunity. The experience is a constantly evolving and widely impacted set of variables that defines "who" you are as an organization and defines the "how and what" your customers can expect from their interaction with you.

How you do business

Your targeting and customer focus will likely change and evolve as your market shifts and your customer base reacts to those shifts. Your constant evaluation of profitability, generations and competition will impact the focus of your targeting and emphasis.

Being a major part of senior management and the leading agent of change within the institution requires a focus on ROI and the budget allocation and use process. You will need to evaluate your budget procedures, the allocation of resources, and the emphasis placed on various aspects of your marketing function.

Looking outward and inward will ensure that you maintain a balance and emphasis on alignment for the organization within its market. You look outward at the marketplace and the competition. And you look inward at your processes, strengths and delivery. The brand promise must align with your institution's strengths as well as the needs of the customer, and fit within an available niche in the marketplace. All such areas are constantly evolving and shifting and require your consistent and meaningful review and analysis.

Communications within the organization will need to be broad, meaningful and consistent. Consistent internal communications provide a fabric that is woven throughout the organization and provide a backdrop for keeping employees abreast of the goals, challenges and focus of the institution. Communications must be delivered to all areas of the bank and provide a level of detail that creates focus and pertinence in order to ensure engagement.

Managing Change

As the leader and agent of change, your role must address the constant flow of change. Some changes require immediate analysis, strategic decisions and tactical implementation. Others simply require ongoing monitoring. You must know the difference and categorize issues, challenges, and shifts to the appropriate decision-making areas of the bank. Change should be managed to be a constant and consistent flow as opposed to periodic large waves of upheaval.

Chapter Keys:

1. Change is present within the industry and change needs to be within your organization; however, change, with purpose, is the desired result
2. Your role, along with everyone's within the institution, will change and the resulting delivery and involvement will also evolve
3. Managing change is fundamental to your success

CHAPTER 18

Bringing It All Together

"Perseverance is not a long race; it is many short races one after another."

- Walter Elliott

As a financial marketer, you have clear challenges ahead of you and critical accountabilities to accept. But success is ultimately within your reach. Every challenge you face represents an opportunity to make a definable difference for your institution and for your career.

Throughout our book, *Shift Happens*, we have outlined areas of change that reflect the dynamic nature of the industry and the marketplace. There's an old adage that states that "the only constant is change." Against that backdrop you must have the fortitude to maintain a process-driven approach to create a marketing function and purpose that drives the organization forward.

Challenges

The challenges of a financial marketer are numerous and include your need to be an agent of change and the need for marketing to evolve into a philosophy at your institution. You must address these fundamental issues with vigor, focus and determination as they will maximize your impact to the organization and propel you forward. Other challenges include:

- Gaining a seat at the executive table
- Maintaining a clear focus on ROI
- Converting information into actionable knowledge
- Integrating planning and research into everyday actions

Accountabilities

Your role includes accountabilities to the organization and to the function of marketing. For your organization, your accountabilities include leveraging your budget, targeting your efforts, supporting the entire organization and the bottom-line results.

For the function of marketing, accountability involves the level of engagement you earn and create within the institution. As we have discussed throughout the book, engagement of the entire bank is mission critical for marketing to take root and become a primary driver of success.

Success

Success will take the form of many different actions and variables that have been thoughtfully considered, managed and implemented. Success for a financial marketer will include:
- Clear brand position and promise
- Articulated targeting
- Strategic communication plan
- Leveraged budget that includes ROI analysis

The Future

As Greg Dufour so eloquently stated in the foreword to this book, "While surviving this period of radical change is imperative, the critical factor to thriving during this period is to develop a network of material that you can personally use to position your organization for the future."

The future clearly begins with you! But it is a future that is bright and full of opportunities for success. Financial marketing has never been more difficult, yet it has never offered a greater chance for success and recognition!

Chapter Keys:

1. Analyze the shifts in your market, institution, customer base and staff to ensure you are attentive to the necessary steps to stay ahead
2. Focus on having a process-driven approach
3. Follow the keys for marketer success

SOURCES

IBM Corporation, *Unlocking Customer Advocacy in Retail Banking: The Customer Focused Enterprise*, IBM Global Services, Somers, NY, 2006

Pine, B. Joseph and Gilmore, James H., *The Experience Economy: Work Is Theatre & Every Business A Stage*, Harvard Business School Press, Boston, MA, 1999

Camus, Albert, *The Myth of Sisyphus*, Alfred A. Knopf, Inc, New York, NY, 1955

Gladwell, Malcolm, *The Tipping Point*, Little, Brown and Company, New York, NY, 2000

Aaker, David A., Building Strong Brands, The Free Press, New York, NY, 1996

Financial Insights, *Customer Metrics Survey: A Quantitative Analysis of Effective Customer Strategies*, Framingham, MA, 2004

Gray, Patricia B, *A Banker Who Makes House Calls*, Fortune Small Business, March 7, 2008

RECOMMENDED READING GUIDE

Advertising

Burns, Thomas J., *Effective Communications and Advertising for Financial Institutions*. Prentice-Hall, 1986.

Dru, Jean-Marie, *Disruption: Overturning Conventions and Shaking Up the Marketplace*. John Wiley & Sons, 1996.

Geller, Lois K., *Response! The Complete Guide to Profitable Direct Marketing*. Oxford University Press, 2002.

Griffin, Jack, *The Do-It-Yourself Business Promotions Kit*. Prentice-Hall Trade Publications, 1995.

Janal, Daniel S., *Online Marketing Handbook: How to Promote, Advertise and Sell Your Products and Services on the Internet*. Van Nostrand Reinhold Trade Publications, 1997.

Shaver, Dick, *The Next Step in Database Marketing: Consumer Guided Marketing: Privacy for Your Customers, Record Profits for You*. John Wiley & Sons, 1996.

Vitale, Joe, Cyberwriting: *How to Promote Your Product or Service Online (Without Being Flamed)*. AMACOM, 1996.

Business (of Banking, and General Business)

Bollenbacher, George M., *The New Business of Banking*. Irwin Professional, 1995.

Brown, Albert J., Jr., *The High Performance Bank: Insights and Advice on How to Make Your Bank a Consistent Top Performer*. Probus, 1994.

DeBonis, J. Nicholas, and Roger S. Peterson, *AMA Handbook for Managing Business to Business Marketing Communications*. NTC Business Books, 1997.

Drucker, Peter F., *Management: Tasks, Responsibilities, Practices.* Harper Business, 1993.

Goldstein, Douglas, and Joyce Flory, T*he Online Business Atlas: The Best Online Sites, Resources and Services in: Management Marketing and Promotion, Sales, Entrepreneurial Ventures.* Irwin Professional, 1996.

Hunter, Victor L., and David Tietyin, *Business to Business Marketing: Creating a Community of Customers.* NTC Business Books, 1997.

Levinson, Jay Conrad, *Guerrilla Marketing: Secrets for Making Big Profits from Your Small Business.* Houghton Mifflin, 1998.

McArthur, C. Dan, and Larry Womack, *Outcome Management: Redesigning Your Business Systems to Achieve Your Vision.* Quality Resources, 1995.

Peters, Thomas J., and Robert H. Waterman, Jr., *In Search of Excellence: Lessons from America's Best-Run Companies.* Harper & Row, 1982.

Wing, Michael J., *The Arthur Andersen Guide to Talking with Your Customers: What They Will Tell You about Your Business When You Ask the Right Questions.* Upstart, 1997.

Distribution Strategies

A Guide to Selecting Bank Locations. American Bankers Association, 1968.

Bennett, Rex O., *Bank Location Analysis: Techniques and Methodology.* American Bankers Association, 1975.

Komenar, Margo, *Electronic Marketing.* John Wiley & Sons, 1996.

Littlefield, James E., G. Jackson Burney, and William V. White, *Bank Branch Location: A Handbook of Effective Technique and Practice.* Bank Marketing Association, 1973.

Seibert, Paul, *Facilities Planning and Design for Financial Institutions: A Strategic Management Guide.* Irwin Professional, 1996.

Future of Banking

Hamel, Gary, and C.K. Prahalad, *Competing for the Future: Breakthrough Strategies for Seizing Control of Your Industry and Creating the Markets of Tomorrow.* Harvard Business School Press, 1994.

Marketing Planning

Bayne, Kim M., *The Internet Marketing Plan: A Practical Handbook for Creating, Implementing and Assessing Your Online Presence.* John Wiley & Sons, 1997.

Hensel, James S., "The Essential Nature of the Marketing Management Process: An Overview," in Leonard L. Berry and L. A. Capaldini, eds., *Marketing for the Bank Executive.* Petrocelli Books, 1974.

Hodges, Luther H., Jr., and Rollie Tillman, Jr., *Bank Marketing: Text and Cases.* Addison-Wesley, 1968.

Joselyn, Robert W., and D. Keith Humphries, *An Introduction to Bank Marketing Planning.* American Bankers Association, 1974.

Ries, Al, and Jack Trout, *Marketing Warfare*, McGraw-Hill, 1997.

Ries, Al, and Jack Trout, *The 22 Immutable Laws of Marketing: Violate Them at Your Own Risk.* HarperCollins, 1993.

Solomon, Michael R., and Elnora W. Stuart, *Marketing: Real People, Real Choices.* Prentice-Hall, 2002.

Stanton, William J., and Charles Futrell, *Fundamentals of Marketing, 8th edition.* McGraw-Hill, 1987.

Marketing Research

Berry, Michael J.A., and Gordon Linoff, *Data Mining Techniques: For Marketing, Sales and Customer Support*. John Wiley & Sons, 1997.

Heslop, Janet (editor), *American Marketplace: Demographics and Spending Patterns, 6th edition.* New Strategist Publications, 2003.

Pol, Louis G., and Richard K. Thomas, *Demography for Business Decision Making*. Quorom Books, 1997.

Pope, Jeffrey L., *Practical Marketing Research*. American Marketing Association, 1993.

Schoner, Bertram, *Marketing Research, Information Systems and Decision Making, 2nd edition*. R.E. Krieger Pub. Co., 1981.

Smith, J. Walker, and Ann S. Clurman, *Rocking the Ages: The Yankelovich Report of Generational Marketing.* HarperBusiness,1998.

Positioning

Ries, Al, and Jack Trout, *Positioning: The Battle for Your Mind.* McGraw-Hill, 2000.

Trout, Jack, T*he New Positioning: The Latest on the World's #1 Business Strategy*. McGraw-Hill, 1997.

Vandermerwe, Sandra, *The Eleventh Commandment: Transforming to 'Own' Customers*. John Wiley & Sons, 1996.

Pricing

Moebs, G. Michael, and Eva Moebs, *Pricing Financial Services*. Dow Jones– Irwin, 1986.

Product Development

Bobrow, Edwin E., *The Complete Idiot's Guide to New Product Development*. MacMillan General Reference, 1997.

Effective Bank Product Management: How to Be Profitable in a Competitive Environment. Bank Administration Institute, 1988.

Patrick, Jerry, *How to Develop Successful New Products*. NTC Business Books, 1997.

Thygerson, Kenneth J., *Product-Line Performance Evaluation Systems for Financial Depositories*. Quorom Books, 1997.

Public Relations

Shiva, V.A., *The Internet Publicity Guide: How to Maximize Your Marketing and Promotion in Cyberspace*. Allworth Press, 1997.

Selling and Sales Management

Alexander, James A., and Michael C. Lyons, *The Knowledge-Based Organization: Four Steps to Increasing Sales, Profits and Market Share*. Irwin Professional, 1995.

Baron, Gerald R., *Friendship Marketing's Salt Principles: Seasoning the Business of Life*. Quest Enterprise Institute, 1997.

Berry, Leonard L., David R. Bennett, and Carter W. Brown, *Service Quality: A Profit Strategy for Financial Institutions*. Dow Jones–Irwin, 1989.

Bly, Robert W., *Secrets of Successful Telephone Selling: How to Generate More Leads, Sales, Repeat Business and Referrals by Phone*. Henry Holt, 1997.

Crosby, John V., *Managing the Big Sale: A Relational Approach to Marketing Strategies, Tactics and Selling.* NTC Publishing Group, 1996.

Graham, John R., *203 Ways to Be Supremely Successful in the New World of Selling.* Simon and Schuster MacMillan, 1996.

Khandpur, Navtej, and Jasmine Wevers, *Sales Force Automation Using Web Technologies.* John Wiley & Sons, 1997.

Lewis, Herschell Gordon, and Robert D. Lewis, *Selling on the Net: The Complete Guide.* NTC Business Books, 1996.

Maslow, A.H., *Motivation and Personality.* Harper Collins Publishers, 1987.

McCloskey, Larry A., and Bryan Wirth. *Selling with Excellence: A Quality Approach for Sales Professionals.* American Society for Quality Press, 1995.

Peppers, Don, and Martha Rogers, Ph.D., *Enterprise One to One: Tools for Competing in the Interactive Age.* Currency/ Doubleday, 1997.

Peppers, Don, and Martha Rogers, Ph.D., *The One to One Future: Building Relationships One Customer at a Time.* Currency/ Doubleday, 1997.

Sterne, Jim, *Customer Service on the Internet: Building Relationships, Increasing Loyalty, and Staying Competitive.* John Wiley & Sons, 2000.

Stowell, Daniel M., *Sales, Marketing, and Continuous Improvement: Six Best Practices to Achieve Revenue Growth and Increase Customer Loyalty.* Jossey- Bass, 1997.

Webster, Frederick E., Jr., and Yoram Wind, *Organizational Buying Behavior.* Prentice- Hall, 1972.

Strategic Marketing and Planning

Beemer, C. Britt, and Robert L. Shook, *Predatory Marketing: What Everyone in Business Needs to Know to Win Today's American Consumer.* William Morrow, 1997.

Hall, Robert E., *The Streetcorner Strategy for Winning Local Markets.* Performance Press, 1994.

Kerin, Roger A., and Robert A. Peterson, *Strategic Marketing Problems: Cases and Comments.* Prentice-Hall, 2003.

Kremer, John, and J. Daniel McComas, *High Impact Marketing on a Low-Impact Budget: 101 Strategies to Turbo-Charge Your Business Today.* Prima, 1997.

Lewis, T.G., Ph.D., *The Friction-Free Economy: Marketing Strategies for a Wired World.* Harper Business, 1997.

Lovelock, Christopher H. and Jochen Wirtz, *Services Marketing.* Prentice-Hall, 2003.

McKitterick, J.B., *The Frontiers of Marketing Thought.* American Marketing Association, 1957.

Vavra, Terry G., *Aftermarketing: How to Keep Customers for Life through Relationship Marketing.* Irwin Professional, 1995.

Violano, Michael, and Shimon-Craig Van Collie, *Retail Banking Technology: Strategies and Resources That Seize the Competitive Advantage.* John Wiley & Sons, 1992.

Target Market Selection/ Segmentation
Best, Roger J., *Market-Based Management: Strategies for Growing Customer Value and Profitability.* Prentice-Hall, 1999.

Gerber, Jerry, Janet Wolff, Walter Klores, and Gene Brown, *LifeTrends: The Future of Baby Boomers and Other Aging Americans.* Simon & Schuster, 1990.

Morgan, Carol M., and Doran J. Levy, Ph.D., *Segmenting the Mature Market: Identifying, Targeting and Reaching America's Diverse, Booming Senior Markets*. Probus, 1993.

Ritchie, Karen, *Marketing to Generation X*. Free Press, 2002.

Sharp, Kevin, and Daniel Johnson, *Know Thy Customer: How to Follow Marketing's First Commandment*. Dartnell, 1997.

Stanley, Thomas J., *Marketing to the Affluent*. McGraw-Hill, 1997.

Rossman, Marlene L., *Multicultural Marketing: Selling to a Diverse America*. AMACOM, 1996.

Trives, Jonathan, *One Stop Marketing*. John Wiley & Sons, 1996.

OTHER RECOMMENDED READING

Loyalty and Customer Service

The Loyalty Effect, Frederick Reicheld, Harvard Business School Press
Loyalty.com, Frederick Newell, McGraw Hill
Blue Ocean Strategy, Kim Mauborgne, Harvard Business School Press
On Great Service, Leonard L. Berry, Free Press
Hug Your Customers, Jack Mitchell, Hyperion

Segmented Marketing

The One to One Future: Building Relationships One Customer at a Time, Don Peppers and Martha Rodgers, Currency/Doubleday

Selling to a Segmented Market, Chester A. Swenson, NTC Business Books

Customer Insight

Value-Based Marketing, Doyle
Think Like Your Customer, Stinnett
Clued In – How to Keep Customers Coming Bank Again and Again, Carbone
How to Become a Rainmaker, Fox

Marketing Financial Services Organizations

Advertising Mail Marketing Association
3252 F Street NW, Suite 362
Washington, DC 20004-1108

Advertising Research Federation
641 Lexington Avenue
New York, NY 10022
212-751-5656

American Advertising Federation
1101 Vermont Avenue NW, Suite 500
Washington, DC 20005
202-898-0089

American Association of Advertising
Agencies
405 Lexington Avenue
New York, NY 10174-1801
212-682-2500

American Bankers Association
1120 Connecticut Avenue NW
Washington, DC 20036
202-663-5000

American Marketing Association
311 South Wacker Drive, Suite 5800
Chicago, IL 60606
312-542-9000

ABA Bank Marketing Network
1120 Connecticut Avenue NW
Washington, DC 20036
202-663-5422

Business Marketing Association
400 N. Michigan Avenue
Chicago, IL 60611
312-822-0005

Direct Marketing Association
212-391-9683

Marketing Science Institute
617-491-2060

Media Dynamics
18 East 41st Street
New York, NY 10017
212-683-7895

National Automated Clearing House Association
13665 Dulles Technology Drive
Herndon, VA 20171

Promotion Marketing Association of America, Inc.
257 Park Avenue South, 11th Floor
New York, NY 10010
212-420-1100

Public Relations Society of America
212-460-1400

Sales and Marketing Executives International
PO Box 1390
Sumas, WA 98295-1390
770-661-8500

Bank Directories

http://www.aaadir.com
AAAdir World Bankshttp://www.cybertechnic.com/eye-on/
yAlphaBanking.html
Eye-On Banking

http://192.147.69.47/drs
FDIC Institution Directory System

http://www.financial-net.com
Financial Net

http://www.f-test.com
Findex

http://www.ffiec.gov/nic/default.HTM
National Information Center of Banking Information

Directories of Bank Web Sites
http:www.aba.com
American Bankers Association, ABA
Member Bank Web Sites

http://www.banksite.com
BankSITE Global Directory

http://www.orcc.com/banking.htm
Online Banking and Financial Services Directory

ABOUT THE AUTHORS

Bruce A. Clapp, CFMP

Bruce is President of MarketMatch, Inc. an Englewood, OH company. MarketMatch provides consulting to financial institutions for marketing strategy, service and sales, marketing delivery, and product development. Prior to starting MarketMatch, Bruce was an executive marketer for several financial institutions ranging in size from $120 million to a $4 billion affiliate of a $100 billion dollar bank. In 2005, Bruce authored the textbook Marketing Financial Services: Building a Better Bank. The textbook was published by the American Bankers Association for use across the country in education and training bank marketers to excel in marketing and promoting their financial institutions and has become the defacto textbook on bank marketing fundamentals.

Bruce is on the teaching faculty of the ABA School of Bank Marketing and the ABA Stonier Graduate School of Banking. Additionally, Bruce has a regular column on Retention and Attrition in the ABA Bank Marketing magazine and is a frequent contributor of articles and a cited expert in many articles for trade publications around the country. Bruce can be reached at baclapp@MarketMatch.com

Nick Vaglio, CFMP

Nick Vaglio, a Certified Financial Marketing Professional (CFMP), is Vice President of Commercial Marketing for Wachovia Bank. He served as the Chair (2004-2007) of the Advisory Board for the American Bankers Association's (ABA) Marketing Conference and as the 2008 Chair of the ABA National Marketing Network Council. Nick is a graduate of the ABA School of Bank Marketing and Management. He is the Curriculum Director and lead instructor for the Bank Marketing and Management Forum that is held annually in the Middle East in cooperation between the ABA and the Arab Academy of Banking and Financial Sciences. He has also presented at the 12th Annual

International Banking Conference in Amman, Jordan, and has lectured on marketing at Temple University and at numerous ABA Bank Marketing Network chapters. His articles have appeared in the ABA's Bank Marketing Magazine.

A member of the United States Track and Field Masters Division, he is consistently ranked in the Top 5 in the United States in the high hurdles where he has earned Masters All American honors. Nick can be reached at nvaglio@yahoo.com.

Read 5/18/13

Made in the USA
Charleston, SC
23 February 2012